GAR3

Yale's
SELECTIVE BOOK

Report of a three year project
directed by John H. Ottemiller,
Associate University Librarian,
under a grant from the
Council on Library Resources, Inc.

RETIREMENT PROGRAM

Prepared by
LEE ASH
EDITOR AND RESEARCH ANALYST

ARCHON BOOKS
1963

Published for the Yale University Library by
The Shoe String Press, Inc.
Hamden 14, Connecticut, U.S.A.

CONTENTS

PREFACE

At the conclusion of the three-year study project of Yale's Selective Book Retirement Program, I take the occasion to thank the Council on Library Resources, Inc., once again, for the grant which made the Program possible. We have learned a great deal that we did not know before. Although we believe that our Selective Book Retirement offers a palliative to the increasing space problem in research libraries, we recognize that it is not a solution.

The following brief report, abstracted from a longer report and a series of charts and graphs by the Program's Editor and Research Analyst, Lee Ash, and revised by members of the library staff, is based upon extensive and detailed studies made at Yale during the three years of the Program's duration. The working papers are on file for study by anyone who wishes to see them. As Librarian of the University, in agreement with the Associate University Librarian, John H. Ottemiller, Director of the Selective Book Retirement Program, and also in agreement with the Department Heads of the Library, I believe that this summary report will be of greater interest to administrators of libraries than would the tedious detail of graphs and statistics which accompany the studies we have made.

I also wish to thank the Trustees of Yale University, the Yale Library Committee and the staff of the Selective Book Retirement Program for their help. I appreciate, too, the cooperation of the faculty and students during the period in which we inflicted our interests, questionnaires, and interviews upon them.

James T. Babb
University Librarian

FOREWORD

In granting funds to the Yale University Library for a three-year expansion and study of its Selective Book Retirement Program, the Council on Library Resources specified the following objectives:[1]

"(a) To expedite the Yale University Library's Selective Retirement Program (from 20,000 to 60,000 volumes per year) and to extend it to other libraries on the campus;

(b) To study (in collaboration with the faculty) the bases of selection for retirement for various subjects and forms of material;

(c) To study the effects of the Program on library use and research by faculty, graduate and undergraduate students;

(d) To ascertain what arrangements may compensate for the loss of immediate access caused by the Program;

(e) To explore the possible effectiveness of the Program toward stabilizing the size of the immediate-access collection;

(f) To publish for the use of other libraries the policies, procedures, and results thus discovered."

The study has carried out all of these objectives except (d): "To ascertain what arrangements may compensate for the loss of immediate access caused by the Program." Although there has been some consideration of the supplemental use of printed book catalogues of collections, no information of value was gathered on this point. Some thought has been given to the advisability of retaining in the shelf list a record of books removed to storage, thus giving a classified approach to the material, even though the books have been removed from the shelves. Unfortunately this would mean

[1] Letter from Verner Clapp, February 24, 1959.

classifying all new acquisitions which are assigned directly to storage, thus nullifying the savings resulting from not having to classify these books. Some compensation for the loss of immediate access may also result if academic personnel are better trained in the bibliography and history of their fields and if the preparation and publication of more bibliographies is encouraged.

Our experience has indicated that a library attempting restrictive growth projects or a rearrangement of collections must see that everyone who will be affected by such a program understands its purpose. It is not enough to outline the idea and to secure the approval and commitment of the library committee or trustees on the basis of an early briefing. These people, and the professional library staff particularly, must all be made to feel a part of any new approach to library economy.

It is always difficult to promote a pioneering effort, although any explanation of such a project will find agreeable and interested listeners at the beginning; but one session or one or two memoranda of explanation are not sufficient. A well-planned and continuing program of publicity is requisite. Failure to communicate the desirability of such a program, from the time of its inception till its completion, will limit its maneuverability in terms of helpful cooperation at all levels within an institution.

If administrators of projects like Yale's could avoid the use of such negative phrases and words as "Selective Book Retirement Program," "seldom-used scholarly books," "storage," "discarding," and "obsolescence," it would probably make faculty and staff less apprehensive of the removal of publications from a library's active, open-access collection. We must admit, however, that we have failed to find adequate substitutes for these terms. Professor Frederick A. Pottle has suggested the title "Program of Discard and Selective Transfer to Closed Stacks."

The program has been of real value to Yale in planning the development and disposition of its collections; and it is our hope that the findings of the study, reported here, will prove helpful to other large research libraries. It has pointed up problems in the administration of such a program of which we had not previously been aware; it has provided us with an opportunity to develop improved procedures for handling large-scale transfers from the stacks; and it has given us figures showing the low use of books in the storage collection which corroborate our thinking that a readily accessible storage collection is a sound means of helping to control the growth of a library's active collections.

Perhaps the most effective support of the program within the University is found in the "Report of the University Council Committee on the Library," April 1962. This Committee (Gilbert W. Chapman, Yale '24, Chairman) is a group of persons both from Yale and from outside Yale which studies the development of the Library and advises the University administration and the Yale Corporation on Library programs and policies. The report says (pages 2-3):

"The Council on Library Resources, Inc. supported a Selective Book Retirement Program by a grant of $150,000. This grant expires on June 30, 1962 . . .

"There has been criticism of the retirement program, both from within the Library and from faculty. The men who work in the research 'factories' are particularly concerned. Their great concern is that the retirement program limits the accessibility of books and that the unknown volume will not be found by browsing in the stacks.

"Three times as many books, however, can be shelved in the compact arrangement as in conventional shelving. The criticism of the several locations of books is not valid since the better than four million volumes in the Yale Collections are located in roughly sixty-four different places—in fourteen different places in the Sterling Memorial Library Building. Also, many books are always out anyhow—defeating the aspirations of the browser.

"The Committee is cognizant of criticism but concludes that the project should be continued because of the space problems and further that the weeding will make the open stack collections more usable by the great majority of our readers. The few obsolete and little-used books withdrawn will still be available within Sterling Library through the use of the public catalogue and subject bibliographies."

The Library administration agrees with these statements and is grateful for the understanding and support of this Committee.

I wish to acknowledge the cooperation of members of the Library staff in helping to make the Program a success, in particular, Donald G. Wing, Associate Librarian, who did the major share of book selecting, and F. Bernice Field, Head of the Catalogue Department, and her staff for adjusting to the additional burden of work and the crowding of the work areas resulting from the Program. Special commendation goes to Frances R. Lubovitz, Supervisor in the Catalogue Department of the processing staff for the Program, and her assistants. Miss Lubovitz's ability to develop the procedures of the technical operations is revealed in the detailed manual which she has compiled. I note, also, the useful study of medical theses by Miles Raisig and Frederick G. Kilgour of the Yale Medical Library, summarized in this report, and express my appreciation to Raymond P. Morris, Librarian, Yale Divinity School, for his fine statement on the Program, which we have used to conclude the report. Finally, my gratitude goes to Lee Ash, Editor and Research Analyst, to his team of student assistants, particularly Denis Lorenz, Yale '61, and to the Editorial Committee which reviewed the report: F. Bernice Field, Head, Catalogue Department; J. Gordon Kenefick, Assistant Librarian; Herman W. Liebert, Curator, Rare Book Room; and Donald G. Wing, Associate Librarian. Mr. Hal J. Syren, Library Consultant, was of inestimable help in the work which resulted in the charts and plans on the book stacks reported in chapter 8.

> John H. Ottemiller
> Associate University Librarian
> and Director, Selective Book
> Retirement Program

Yale's SELECTIVE BOOK
RETIREMENT PROGRAM

I

THE SELECTIVE BOOK RETIREMENT PROGRAM

The Selective Book Retirement Program at Yale developed from the need to consider the economic and administrative problems of the rapid growth of the Libraries. The beginning of the storage program in 1943 and its history to the summer of 1959, when operations were expanded under the Council's grant, are reviewed in an article by the Director of the Program, John H. Ottemiller, and his associates, published in the *Yale University Library Gazette* for October 1959. In that article reference is made to the uncontrolled rate of growth of American university and research libraries. It also mentions that, "After ten years of tentative experimentation, the University Librarian, James T. Babb, in his *Report,* 1952-53, took the essential step of formally declaring a radical policy for Yale." This policy was to expand the program which had for ten years been assigning to storage appropriate books from new acquisitions. With the approval of the Yale Corporation it was decided in 1952-53 to initiate a program of selecting books already in the stacks, with the following purposes:

1. To decatalogue and discard material considered to have no further scholarly value, with the advice and counsel of the faculty.

2. To secure in microtext form books, periodicals, and newspapers selected because of infrequent use, bulk, lack of bibliographical importance and condition, and to discard the originals.

3. To transfer from the regular stacks to storage little-used books, arranged by size rather than by subject.

It should be pointed out that for most of its existence the Yale University Library had operated on the principle that it should acquire everything that it could afford to purchase or that was offered as a gift or an exchange. But in the 1950's the Yale

Library, in common with other large libraries, recognized that, with the proliferation of printed materials after the war, it could never provide space to house or staff to process and service such an all-inclusive collection and that it must become more selective in its acquisitions. The Library administration, therefore, began to move toward a clarification of the needs of the Library in light of the University's program of teaching and research and the development of selective acquisition policies.

Because the Library had for years attempted to be a library of record, however, the stacks contained many publications of marginal value in the program of the University, and the Library administrators believed that a careful survey of the collection in the stacks would reveal a considerable amount of material that could be removed to storage, or in some cases discarded, without too much damage to the collections. They hoped that judicious weeding would result in a collection that would be more significant for faculty and students and would save them from having to search through much material of little or no value to find that which was of importance to them. They also thought that by transferring to storage or replacing by microfilm material that showed little use they could make room in the stacks for publications of more importance to present users of the Library.

As of May 31, 1959, there were 104,694 volumes in the storage stacks, accumulating at the average rate of 14,000 volumes a year. An additional 6,000 volumes represented discards, transfers to other libraries, and volumes replaced by microfilm.

But, as Mr. Ottemiller wrote in 1958, ". . . the University is dissatisfied (a) with the rate of transfer [to storage], (b) with its knowledge of the basis on which such transfers are made, and (c) with its knowledge of the effect of its procedures in terms of both efficiency of operation and of service to users.

"It consequently . . . [proposed to the Council on Library Resources] a three-year concentrated program, sufficiently well-guided and controlled so as to make it possible to secure valid data of the following kinds, which would be useful to the University and to other libraries, also; data for improving the criteria of selection for compact storage to be applied to various types of material, both old and current, these to be sought in consultations with the faculty; data on the frequency of the use of various types of material; data with which to test the ever-normal-granary assumption which underlies the present operations; data with which to estimate the optimum size of collection for a university of this character; data on the relationship of the cataloguing apparatus both to the working and the compact collection, on the use of subject cataloguing, etc.; data collected as a result of questionnaires and interviews from faculty and graduate students, as to the use of catalogues, bibliographies, browsing, etc."

The Council on Library Resources made its grant to Yale to help the library accomplish the specific aim of increasing the Selective Book Retirement Program's function of processing from 20,000 to 60,000 volumes a year, thereby providing a body of material large enough to validate statistical data. The Program was to be extended to school and departmental libraries in order to encompass some special studies and to help substantiate, in collaboration with faculty and students, bases of selection of materials for storage, taking into consideration subject, published form, age, frequency of use, etc.

Now, three years later, we are ready to summarize the results. Figures and cost analyses for the removal of books from the main library stacks for storage, transfer or discard are given in Chapter VII of this report. We are satisfied that the speed of processing is greater and the costs considerably lower than are generally estimated for such functions (61 cents per volume processed). The *rate* of removal of material from the stacks has averaged about 48,000-50,000 items per year. The total number of volumes in storage (monographs, serials and dissertations), as of June 30, 1962, is 193,082, of which 88,836 have been put into storage since the project got under way in September 1959. Of this figure, 74,648 volumes were transferred from the main stacks, and 14,188 were new acquisitions catalogued by the regular cataloguing staff. In these three years we have also discarded 28,443 items, of which 6,695 were monographs, 11,087 were serial volumes and 10,661 were pamphlets. These were largely practical duplicates of editions remaining in the Library, cheap reprint editions, volumes in such poor condition that they could not be retained, dissertations that were reprints from periodicals in the Library's collections, scattered volumes of serial titles which appeared to be of little value in a research collection and were available at nearby libraries. Another 17,259 items have been transferred to other libraries, some on campus and others at different institutions.

The Selective Book Retirement Program also encompassed book retirement activities in the Divinity and Medical School Libraries. In addition, it placed in storage many books selected during the integration of five scattered collections into a consolidated Geology Library. Special collections were not generally involved in the Program except as curators might suggest books to be transferred to storage, or as they received transfers from the Main Library stacks in the course of selecting titles for storage.

II

SELECTION OF MATERIAL FOR STORAGE: POLICIES AND PROBLEMS

By discussion and questionnaire, we have sought the bases of selection for storage of materials in certain subject fields and in certain forms. This has required a consideration of the Library's acquisitions policies, a study of publications at the shelves, and an investigation of the use of storage books by the Library's patrons.

This chapter will describe the efforts to develop, in consultation with faculty, principles of selecting material for removal from the stacks and the problems encountered. Chapters III and IV will give the results of two special studies on problems of selection. The analysis of readers' use of books in the storage collection is discussed in Chapter V.

WEEDING POLICIES

General Policies

Prior to the expansion of the Selective Book Retirement Program in 1959, the Library, in assigning publications to storage, had followed certain general principles developed by the Head of the Catalogue Department, which had been codified in the Department Manual under the heading: *W (Storage) Collection.* These principles specified types of material which are generally assigned to storage, types which should be considered for storage, and material which should not be put in storage.

Early in the first year of the expanded Program, because of questions which came from the project staff in the Catalogue Department, general principles relating to the weeding of editions and copies were also codified for the *Manual* under the heading: *W (Storage) Collection. Selection: Policies, General.* These two documents helped to solve many problems for the SBRP professional staff in the Catalogue Department.

At the end of the three-year Program, the Head of the Catalogue Department, drawing upon both the experience gained in selecting and processing the material during the period and upon her knowledge of policies followed by the Library, coordinated and expanded these documents to include policies for discarding on which the Library administration had agreed at various times, policies for transferring material to the major school and departmental libraries, and other principles of weeding which were followed in the Library but which had not hitherto been written down except, in some cases, in separate memoranda. The resulting document, SELECTIVE BOOK RETIREMENT PROGRAM: PURPOSES AND POLICIES, which is given in the Appendices (pages 71 ff), is a direct result of the Program.

Policies in Subject Fields

General policies were easier to formulate than those applying to specific fields. One of the major problems in the latter area arises because of the cross subject interests of faculty. The geographer, for example, depending on his field of specialization, may be interested in demography, industrial development, transportation, ethnography, political science, international relations, agriculture, human and physical resources, oceanography, marine geology, conservation, etc. The historian may be interested in economics, description and travel, population movements, industries, political science, international relations, etc. The scientists and mathematicians have many interlocking interests. The catholicity of subject interests among the faculty of a large university makes it difficult to set up even broad guide lines for weeding in subject areas.

In a university or college of today the very nature of the teaching program will probably inhibit the development of definitions of books that are useful in given subject areas. It proved easier at Yale to recommend specific *titles* for withdrawal from the stacks than specific *groups* or *types* of material within a subject field. These were selected by studying the books at the shelves;

and decisions were based on the value of a title as subject matter or its importance historically in the field, the availability of other editions and other material on the subject, the use the volume had received, its physical condition, etc.

Furthermore, because faculty members and librarians approach weeding from different points of view, it is difficult for them to agree on policies of selection in a subject field. The faculty members consider publications chiefly as they relate to the subject in which their interests lie, while the librarian must take a much broader view. He must keep in mind the library's collecting policies and the over-all development of the library's collections. He must know the strengths and weaknesses of the library in various subject fields and the interests of the special collections in the library. He must be aware of new programs which the university has undertaken as well as established ones. He must consider the bibliographical importance of publications, the relative expense of processing certain forms of material for a storage collection versus keeping them in the stacks. On the other hand, policies for selection based solely on the librarian's criteria have resulted in criticism by faculty of some of the books allocated to storage at Yale.

Perhaps the best policy is for librarians to make the first selection of candidates for storage and, having informed the faculty as to the meaning of a storage program, its necessity, its advantages, and the accessibility of stored books, to ask for the approval of the major department concerned. It is not easy, however, to find faculty who have the time or interest to cooperate fully in such a procedure. Occasionally some of them will assist; but, in general, they seem to feel that both acquisition and selection for storage are the province of the librarian.

Transfer of Entire Subject Groups to Storage

If we could not agree on policies for selection of materials within a subject group for transfer to storage, could we find subject groups that could be moved to storage *en masse* without volume by volume weeding, as is so often suggested? This was the next question we investigated. In every area studied, however, we found material that was heavily used (a criterion for keeping it in the stacks), incomplete and current serials, pamphlets, material in too poor condition or of too little value to be retained in the Library. Our experience seemed to prove that at Yale, at least, assignment to storage cannot be done on this basis; in fact, it reinforced our belief that satisfactory weeding can be done only by examining the books themselves.

Policies for Serials

Agreement on a sound policy for the transfer of serials to storage also eluded us. In planning the expanded Selective Book Retirement Program we had expected that serials, especially long, complete serial sets and early long runs of currently published serials, would constitute a major part of the transfers, and our processing staff had been planned on this premise. To our surprise we encountered considerable opposition to moving this type of material out of the open-access collections into closed-stacks storage.

Faculty members were reluctant to transfer long serial sets to storage, particularly if there were no cumulative index to them. They said that faculty and students like to search through such material, and often from this come ideas for papers or dissertations or new angles on topics of great interest to their research. Those working on various editorial projects in the Library did not want anything to go to storage and especially not serials. The Reference Department staff objected to the transfer of any of the learned society serial publications to storage because of the heavy use they receive; further transfer of these was, therefore, suspended until the Research Analyst could undertake a study of their use (see next chapter).

Incomplete serial files proved to be an even bigger problem. Since the Yale storage collection allows no space for additions, we could not put incomplete serials into it. Yet to weeders these were prime candidates for storage. We reviewed this problem from every angle but found no satisfactory answer. We agreed that, if not more than ten per cent of the volumes of a set were lacking, we would transfer the set to storage and put boxes on the shelves in place of the missing volumes so that there would be space for them if received. If more than fifty per cent of the set were lacking, we considered whether it should be discarded, whether it should be transferred to another library to fill its gaps, or whether we should try to fill in the gaps or replace the entire set by microfilm. But seldom were volumes to fill the lacks or a microfilm available. If a complete set for filming was located in some other library, usually the cost of a single copy was too high for its potential use in the University. Occasionally we decided to put an incomplete file in storage if nothing had been added to the set in years and it seemed unlikely to have additions in the future. In so doing, we took the risk of having to relocate the set or add a second call number if volumes were received later. The problem of incomplete serials in relation to compact storage has not been solved.

If Yale had a separate storage library, with ample shelving space, the Head of the Catalogue Department would recommend that incomplete serial files which are considered to be storage material be tranferred but not incorporated into the files of material in compact storage, since this kind of shelving allows no room for adding volumes. A section of the storage stacks could be set aside for these, which would allow space for additions, and the sets would retain their present call numbers. Instead of withdrawing the catalogue cards and changing the call numbers, the Catalogue Department would stamp the cards "Storage" above the call number. This would rid the stacks of a large amount of relatively unimportant material and would cause no problem if volumes were received for adding. If a set in this area were completed, it could then be transferred to compact storage. Present space for the collection does not permit this, however.

WEEDING PROBLEMS

In addition to difficulties in securing agreement on policies for selecting material for withdrawal from the stacks, we encountered problems in what might be called the mechanics of weeding which we had not anticipated.

Lack of Regularity in Weeding
Foremost was the problem of finding enough faculty and staff to select 4,000 to 5,000 volumes per month for removal from the stacks and keeping those assigned to it on the regular schedules of work that were necessary to insure a steady flow of work to the processing staff in the Catalogue Department.

Although the grant from the Council on Library Resources provided funds for paying faculty to weed at the rate of five dollars per hour, it proved impossible for them to work on a regular schedule. In the beginning each man, recommended by his department head, welcomed the opportunity to survey the collection. But faculty are busy people; and, no matter how keen their interest, they were forced to default in their time because of other commitments, research, advisory service to government or private organizations, or, very frequently, "the finishing of my book for which the galleys have just come." In only a few cases were the men able to continue to the end of their assignment.

It becomes more and more apparent that a library can depend upon faculty members to assist in book retirement or in book selection only in rare cases; and increasingly, as one talks with faculty, one hears their insistent suggestion that these tasks are the librarian's job, that it is an imposition to expect a teacher to take on a librarian's job, that one engaged in research can make only specific suggestions with regard to his own needs.

The most satisfactory solution seems to be the addition to library staffs of subject bibliography specialists whose scholarship and cooperation with faculty will develop between the librarians and faculty a sense of mutual dependency and respect.

One of the by-products of using faculty for selecting materials to be retired from the stacks was the evidence, seen at first hand and freely admitted by younger faculty members, of the inadequate training that faculty have had in the bibliography and history of their fields. This limited knowledge may tend to narrow the scope of their understanding of publications in their subject fields, which is necessary for making valid decisions in the selection process. This situation does not exist only at Yale; it has been recognized by many writers in recent years.

A survey of one hundred humanities and seventy-seven social science faculty members of all ranks at Yale brought mostly negative responses to the questions: "Did your training include courses in the reference materials of your discipline? Did your graduate work include, either in special courses or by way of seminars, specific training in the use of bibliographical tools in your field? Can you describe the way in which you learned to use such aids?" Almost all of the men replied, essentially, that their training had been a hit-or-miss experience; less than five per cent of these men answered those questions affirmatively.

Diminishing Returns Over a Long Period

A second problem in a long-range weeding program is that the longer such a program exists, the more difficult the process becomes. In the beginning a library naturally selects for review those subject areas which are of little importance to the college or university program of teaching and research or in which the major interest rests with another library in the university library system, and the amount of material that can be removed from the stacks is high. As those subjects are completed, the selecting becomes more time-consuming and difficult; and, as the staff moves to subjects that are heavily used, hours of work produce but meager results.

At Yale, for example, the weeding of such subjects as agriculture and domestic science brought high returns for the time expended because the University has no strong interest in these fields. The same was true of medicine and theology, in which the University has major school libraries responsible for developing the research collections in these fields. But, when we worked on economics, we found very little material to transfer to storage and practically none to discard.

It should also be mentioned that it was easier to maintain a high rate of withdrawal of material from the stacks during the first year than later because there were sections of the stacks that had been selected for transfer to storage prior to 1959 but had not been handled because of staff limitations. These were sections which required no volume-by-volume weeding, for it had been agreed that all volumes should go to storage, namely, dissertation files in economics, sociology, chemistry, physics and technology, and a shorthand collection. It should be noted that, with the exception of the shorthand collection, these were materials arranged by type within a subject group rather than a whole subject class.

By the second year the weeding of the areas of low interest to the Library had been completed, the transfer of the dissertation files except for those in the field of science had been finished, and the selecting began to go more slowly.

The "Ever-Normal-Granary" Theory

One of the purposes of the Selective Book Retirement Program was to test the "ever-normal-granary" theory as applied to the growth of collections; in other words, can a library control the growth of its active collection by moving from the stacks each year as many volumes as it adds?

Our experience seems to prove that at Yale, at least, it would be very difficult to do this. The inability to maintain regularity in weeding schedules, and the ever more obvious fact that the longer a weeding program continues the more difficult the selecting process becomes, indicate that a large research library cannot withdraw from the stacks each year as much as it adds. A full-time weeding staff, thoroughly versed in the library's acquisition policies and interests, might be able to accomplish this for a few years; but it seems evident that once the collection has been weeded throughout this rate of withdrawal cannot be continued. If the library assigns current receipts to storage on the same bases as it weeds the collections, the amount of material to be withdrawn will be obviously less.

If, however, a library, because of space problems, must decentralize its stacks collection, it could accomplish this by adopting more drastic and arbitrary policies for removal of material to storage than the Yale Library administration, faced with the opposition of faculty to closed stack storage, was willing to accept. Some libraries might move entire sections of the classification into storage; others might decide to remove all publications prior to a certain date from its stacks; while still others might transfer certain types of publications, such as newspapers and folio-sized periodicals, to the storage collection. Each library faced with such a situation would have to decide on policies which would result in the least inconvenience to its users. Under these assumptions, our experience indicates that the "ever-normal-granary" theory is practical and can be made operative but only if a university administration decides to manage its library facilities according to this principle. This decision must, of course, be predicated upon the size of the library's physical plant, present or future, and the assumption that the open access collection in this plant will be adequate for the institution's teaching and research program.

Disagreement With Weeders

Since the Associate Librarian in charge of book selection at Yale is responsible for the over-all development of the collection and knows the Library's interests better than others who weeded, it was agreed that, in order to prevent serious mistakes, he would review *cards* for titles selected for storage that seemed questionable to the Supervisor of the processing staff in the Catalogue Department and would examine all *books* selected for discarding. A good many times he changed the weeder's recommendations. This leads us to recommend that all weeding be surveyed by a member of the library staff who is fully cognizant of the many facets of a library's interests.

Because some faculty and staff members of the various editorial projects going on in the Library were unhappy about having any material removed from the stacks, we agreed to notify the persons chiefly concerned with the particular subject areas weeded and extend to them and the curators of the special collections the privilege of looking over the shelf list cards and requesting a change in the recommended action. The faculty members of some departments took advantage of this offer; others did not, leaving the decision to us. Editorial staffs and curators displayed an active interest in this and suggested the retention of a considerable number of titles in the stacks. Although this review slows up the processing, it is worthwhile in terms of avoiding errors, and it engenders good will toward the program.

III

SPECIAL STUDIES ON SELECTION OF MATERIALS
FOR STORAGE

I. General Learned Society Serials

The growing mass of those publications designated in the library's classification as general learned society proceedings and journals represents one of the greatest problems of library administration in terms of space and bibliographical control. Some libraries have arbitrarily designated cutoff dates for the retention of such publications in the stacks and have relegated earlier files to a storage area. Selection of candidates for storage has usually depended upon the recommendations of the reference and circulation department staffs; and, while some conflict and argument has always accompanied such decisions, the press of space has tended to force a move to storage. Generally these two departments of a library, frequently in consultation with the catalogue department, have been able to select a convenient arbitrary cutoff date, prior to which volumes would be put into storage, and have chosen the particular titles which would not be put into storage at all, either because they were demonstrably in frequent use or because their readers' principal approach to them must be a visual one; *e.g.,* publications with plates.

At Yale, therefore, when the Director and the Research Analyst of the Selective Book Retirement Program, in agreement with the Head of the Circulation Department, suggested the need for such a decision and pressed for the removal to storage of selected learned society serial publications, the immediate and emphatic opposition of the Library staff to the suggestion was not anticipated. The objections that were raised were subsequently analyzed and have been recorded in the working papers of this Program.

To counter these objections with direct evidence, a one-year study of the circulation of a selected group of these publications at Yale, Harvard, and the New York Public Library was undertaken by the Selective Book Retirement Program. The detailed work done in selecting, qualifying, and measuring comparable factors of the sampling, and the methods applied in the study are set out in the files of the Program at Yale. One of the most interesting and persuasive arguments in favor of storing selected pre-1900 learned society serial publications is presented in the comparable and remarkably uniform percentages of the following table.

Institution	Total Number of Charges in One Year	Pre-1900 Charges	Per Cent of Total
Yale	4,184*	662	15.82
Harvard	748*	133	17.78
New York Public Library	3,562	655	18.38

*Yale figures include only the Main Library; the Harvard figures only the Widener Library.

Unfortunately, in compiling these figures, we did not realize until after the job had been done how much lower the percentages would be if we had excluded from the analysis those much-used serials which *would never be considered as candidates for storage.* Had this been done, each of the figures in the table would be reduced by at least five per cent.

Upon deeper examination, our analysis of the three libraries' circulation of comparable samples of titles (all were checked against the Yale shelf list and only titles held by all three libraries were included in the comparison) reflected an almost identical pattern of use by date, with the greatest use beginning with the decade of the 1930's. The conclusion is that, when measured by date of publication, the general learned society serials of early years are relatively infrequently used, and retirement to storage on a selective basis can include consideration of the date factor as an element for determining titles suitable for such transfer. The language distribution of charges of pre-1900 general learned society serial publications studied at Yale was as follows: English 55.75 per cent; French 18.63 per cent; German 10.6 per cent; all other languages — Cyrillic and Slavic, Italian, Scandinavian, Spanish, Dutch, Latin and Greek — made up the remaining 15 per cent of the total in one year.

On the basis of our measurement of the shelf space occupied by these serials (pre-1900, 4,633 feet) we extended our study to include the years 1900-1925, during which period the rate of borrowing by class of borrowers and language distribution was almost the same as for the pre-1900 serials; these represent an additional 2,141 feet of stack space at Yale. We have no reluctance in suggesting that these pre-1925 books demonstrated to be in infrequent use and occupying 1.23 miles of shelf space should be moved to storage under a not too selective program. It does not seem reasonable, from the administrator's point of view, that a library cannot develop a formula that will alleviate the serious crowding now straining the available stack area.

About 85 per cent of the charges for certain general learned society serial publications are for volumes published after 1900, while about 15 per cent are for materials published before that date. Evidence indicates that, if heavily used serials in the groups studied at the three libraries were to be excluded from the sample (as they would be, since they would certainly not be recommended for storage), these figures would probably be closer to 89 and 11 per cent respectively. On the basis of this evidence we believe that, in the future, blocks of these publications can be considered for storage at intervals representing twenty-five or fifty-year runs without reducing the general efficiency of a large research collection.

In view of the staff reaction to our recommendations at Yale we decided to go beyond this institution in our inquiries. A small but carefully selected and representative sample of librarians at college, university and large public libraries (falling into three groups: circulation librarians, reference librarians, and administrative (chief) librarians) were interviewed for their opinions of the Yale findings.

Circulation Librarians

Short of new buildings, circulation librarians saw no alternative solution for the problem of book stacks overcrowded by the present rate of growth. They agreed that evidence of use of serials studied in this report justified the transfer of such books to storage on a selective basis.

They favored automatic selection by date as the best means of transferring sizable blocks to storage. Recognizing that some problems would arise in adjusting the catalogue record, that some inconveniences and delays might result, and that there would be some reader objections to the breaking up of sets and the curtailment of browsing facilities, they believed that these difficulties would not be so great as generally assumed.

They pointed out that, if storage books are fully catalogued and the circulation staff is adequate, whole sets may be ordered from storage almost as readily as from any closed stack. Their unanimous experience that interlibrary loan calls for pre-1925 books of the classes studied in this report averaged less than two volumes per week led them to dismiss objections against storage on grounds of inconvenience for this class of use.

In summary, circulation librarians agreed that, given critical shortage of space and daily deliveries from convenient storage facilities (within a ten-mile radius), there should be no valid objections to storage of such books on a selective but wide basis.

Reference Librarians

Reference librarians, together with a few cataloguers interviewed, were on the whole opposed to any storage of learned society serials. The strongest expression of this opposition was at Yale.

The opinions on which this opposition rests include the views: that frequent use is made of such materials in the stacks; that they are often used at hours when the storage collection would be closed, by readers who cannot come to the Library at other hours; that broken sets and curtailed browsing would impose a serious handicap on scholarship; that reference department work (of which at Yale it was claimed 25 per cent lay in identifying serials and locating items in learned society publications) would be seriously hampered; and that the trouble and delay of ordering books from storage would interfere with effective interlibrary loan service.

Most of these respondents did not specify the extent to which their objections applied to the pre-1925 materials with which this report deals. Some were willing to accept transfers to storage, but only with a high degree of selectivity, with faculty approval, and as a last resort in the face of space pressure.

Reference librarians also felt that the circulation figure of fifteen per cent for pre-1900 learned society publications represented considerable use by scholars, warranting retention of such materials in the stacks. They believed that use at the shelf was essential and that delay of one or two days in securing material would impose a serious handicap. Recognizing that dated materials are less used in the sciences, they believed that all serials without regard to date or evidence of reader use are required on the open shelf for research in the humanities.

Library Administrators

Library administrators, many of whom have already had to face the need for storage, generally approved both the theoretical conclusions of this report and its practical objectives. All of them agreed that a large research library with acute space problems would have to store part of its collections, and that large blocks of learned society serials could be seriously considered for storage automatically by date. There was some question as to the relative 85:15 per cent figures developed on the project at Yale, but even the most critical believed it to be a "border line figure" and said that, if it could be reduced by the removal of a few key series which would never be recommended for storage, it would then undoubtedly be more significant.

These administrators felt that the storage area must be close to the library and that, if it were not, the problem of storage would take on entirely different proportions and require different approaches. They agreed that, if a storage area were close, and delivery service to the main library efficient, the storage of some materials would not seriously damage the effectiveness of a large research collection. All of them felt that, besides critical gains in available space for more essential works and advantages in storage costs, the main stack collection would also become more manageable for the majority of users.

There was some disagreement as to the problem of the closed stack and the scholar's needs. Some believed that there would be little browsing among pre-1900 materials, since most of them would be adequately covered by bibliographical tools. There is, however, plenty of evidence that physical search through many unindexed serials is always essential, and that bibliographical control of the resources of learned society serial publications is wholly insufficient. The librarians seemed to agree that browsing was most useful among materials of more recent years for which there is inadequate current cataloguing or indexing. The idea was advanced that, for the most part, scholars approach older (pre-1925) material with very specific ideas of what they want. Among the faculty members we interviewed at Yale, this was not the attitude of the men who claimed that they must browse; but, among the large proportion who said that browsing was not necessary to them, this idea was acceptable.

Only the reference librarians seemed to feel that delay between request and deliveries of storage books posed any problem. The administrative librarians were unable to agree with them that this created any unjust inconvenience, especially for any book considered a rational choice for storage. The administrators believed that microreproduction of serials is expensive and foolhardy when *use* is the sole objective. They feel it has been amply established in library literature that extensive microfilming is too costly except when fairly short runs are filmed. The only justifications for it, they agreed, were *preservation* of materials, or the relative likelihood of additional copies having to be duplicated.

Administrative librarians expressed considerable interest in the possibility of classified in preference to compact storage. Such storage, though it would be more expensive, would have the advantage of allowing scholars access to the shelves, eliminating most complaints about storage.

All of the administrators agreed that the problem is one of balance between tangibles and intangibles; the actual amount of space made available in a stack area for more heavily used materials, or the amount of money saved by inexpensive storage facilities, must be weighed against the intangibles of community good will, the exceptional scholarship that comes through finding an unknown book by searching in the stacks, or the time when a scholar must consult a particular work very quickly. Unfortunately this balance cannot be measured either by empirical speculation or by statistics.

IV

SPECIAL STUDIES ON SELECTION OF MATERIALS FOR STORAGE

II. Medical Theses Study

As a part of the Selective Book Retirement Program, L. Miles Raisig, Research Assistant, and Frederick G. Kilgour, Librarian, Yale Medical Library, conducted a study to help determine the future fate of the medical thesis collection and, at the same time, to elicit data helpful for formulating similar decisions concerning other such collections.[1] The study is an attempt to secure practical answers to the problems of storing and processing the Yale collection comprising more than 100,000 European medical theses, mostly published since 1890. On the basis of experience, these dissertations have no current value for student use, for the care of patients, or for the prevention of disease. Their possible value to historical research, their use in the last hundred years, and the need for processing and storing them today have fixed the course of the investigation.

The study was limited to references to dissertations published in periodicals appearing in Ash's *Serial Publications Containing Medical Classics: An Index to Citations in Garrison-Morton.* Every citation in the journals selected was tallied, with each thesis reference recorded separately for its source, author, etc. Citation counts were assembled in a table by journals and source years, and at the completion of the analysis of each journal the percentage of these citations to all citations was plotted on a graph. This chart permitted the ready contrast and comparison of journal

---

[1] The full report of this study was delivered to the Second International Congress on Medical Librarianship, June 16-22, 1963, in Washington, D.C., and is scheduled to be published in the *Bulletin of The Medical Library Association,* January 1964, the Proceedings volume of the Conference.

citations, illustrated periods of greatest citation use, and suggested that the period around 1850 would serve best as a starting point for analysis.

In planning method and procedure, the following basic statistics and records were believed to be of primary importance: recorded source and bibliographical data of the thesis citation (journal, page, year; author, title, university, year of publication); number of total citations, of citations to journal articles, of thesis citations, and of all non-journal citations. As medical journals have served well, by reason of their variety and citation yield, in many previously reported citation analyses, this source was chosen as easily available and most useful. The years 1885-1960, tentatively selected for study, were determined by the Yale Medical Library's thesis collection, and in the belief that this period would probably contain the greatest change in use of theses.

To attain a high degree of objectivity in the choice of source journals, expert statistical counsel was sought on desirable characteristics of the citation population and on sampling and recording techniques. The anticipated infrequency of the dissertation reference required inverse sampling, or full counting, of citations within each selected volume of a source journal. A random pattern of publication year selected was achieved in a planned analysis of volumes dated every eighth or tenth year of some fifteen journals — later reduced because of time limitations to every tenth year in ten journal titles.

Their study of 140,534 references yielded 2,669 citations to 2,452 individual dissertations. The greatest citation use of the medical dissertation was made from about 1880 to 1910. Dissertations cited in this period of heavy use have become a part of the historical record of medicine and appear to have no value other than the historical one, which they clearly possess. Available data point to no more than a token citation use of the dissertation in the present. The obvious conclusion is that, in general, the dissertation of today offers little to the advance of medicine, and, if the trend of recent decades persists, it will add less in the future. Since there is little citation use of the dissertation today, moreover, it follows that it is not becoming a part of the historical record, and, with the exception of the more heavily used Paris theses, has slight research or historical value.

These conclusions are not offered as definite guide lines for the discard, storage or processing of these collections; but it is believed that sufficient data are presented here which, when combined with the facts of local conditions, will make possible sound decisions concerning future maintenance and processing of such collections.

It is clear that the Yale Medical Library should retain its thesis collections for historical use. It is equally clear that only a minimum of time should be expended on acquiring printed (not typewritten), current French and German theses; in fact those not received automatically by exchange will not be sought. In the field of medicine, theses other than French and German should not be acquired.

V

ANALYSIS OF
READERS' USE OF THE STORAGE COLLECTION

In order to gain an understanding of the use by readers of books in the storage collection, the Research Analyst initiated two studies. The first, which aimed at finding out which books in the storage collection were used and who used them, was accomplished through collecting all call slips for books with W call numbers for a period of two years, from the fall of 1959 to the same date in 1961, and analyzing them. The second, which purposed to find out why readers request books from the storage collection and what use they make of them, was carried out by means of a questionnaire that was given to all readers who presented call slips for titles shelved in W.

The full statistical analysis of the call slips and the questionnaires is on file at the Yale University Library. This report will summarize the findings, which will probably not surprise many librarians and will certainly confirm some patterns of use that were previously only suppositions.

ANALYSIS OF CALL SLIPS

The study of the call slips was intended to provide a detailed record of the calls upon the book resources that the Library administration had sent to storage. A count of the number of books used and an analysis of who was using them seemed the most effective way of answering the faculty criticism of a storage program.

In the two-year period during which the call slips were collected, nearly 6,000 volumes of the approximately 180,000 in the storage collection (3⅓ per cent) were requested; these were distributed almost equally, 3,000 for each year. A separate count of individual titles was not kept. This is not very strenuous use of the storage collection; and it should be made clear that, if the books in storage had not been readily available (they are shelved in the basement of the main University Library), the use would have been less.

A table shows the groups from which the 5,791 requests came and the proportion of the users which each group represented:

Summary Analysis of Storage-Book Use
During a Two-Year Period

Users	Charges	Per Cent
Graduate students	1,766	30.49
Undergraduates	1,514	26.14
Faculty	718	12.39
Staff (including "Factories")[1]	651	11.24
Special (including visitors, faculty wives and children)	505	8.72
Unidentified (including illegible charges)	414	7.14
Interlibrary loans	223	3.85
Totals	5,791	99.97+

[1] "Factories" at Yale are special research projects housed in the Sterling Memorial Library which are involved with editorial production, *e.g.,* the Boswell Papers, the Franklin Papers, the Walpole Papers, etc.

The call slips were further analyzed by language, by subject and by date of publication, and we believe that the results would be reflected in similar use at other research libraries. It should be apparent from these findings that the use of storage books at Yale is so limited that problems are not likely to occur in library service.

Use of Storage Books by Language Groups

As would be expected, the analysis of the languages of the books requested from the storage collection showed that books in English rated first for all classes of readers and were in considerable excess of all other languages combined. Books in German ranked second, being the second most frequently called for by graduate students, special users and staff, and third by faculty and undergraduates. Books in the French language were the third most frequently requested, being second among faculty and undergraduates and fourth among the staff. The scattering of other languages and their relevant rank in the scale of use is of little significance.

Interlibrary loans also ranked in the same order — English, German, French, while books in Cyrillic and Slavic languages ranked fourth. Yale has not analyzed its interlibrary loans from the stacks in this way, so there is no measure of comparison between the usual volume of borrowing and that of books from the storage collection.

Use of Storage Books by Subject

Time and personnel limitations on the project prohibited an exact classification by subject of the books represented by the nearly 6,000 call slips. Instead, a rough classification was made of the titles, grouping them into Fine and Applied Arts, Literature, Science, Religion, History, Political Science, Sociology and Serial Publications.

The analysis demonstrates the significantly high proportion of books called for in the fields, listed here by rank, of History, Political Science and Sociology, followed by Fine and Applied Arts. The reason for the demand upon this last class is the necessity for students of art to examine illustrations, such as reproductions of paintings, plates of architectural detail, etc.; this we discovered by direct interviews with over 150 users. It might also be added that, since the Art class has been weeded in its entirety, there is a large number of books in this field in storage.

The figures for Science were very low, and we cannot interpret them except to reflect that several factors probably influence the small number of charges for books in this field: (a) few areas of science have been culled for storage material; (b) studies in the history of science are only now taking on purpose and direction at Yale, with a relatively new Department of the History of Science and Medicine; (c) modern materials in the sciences receive heavier use in every library, and these are not in storage; (d) Yale has departmental libraries in almost every major field of science which bear the brunt of the use of books in this field. Factor (a) means that there are very few books in the field of Science in the storage collection; and, as for factor (b), an examination of who borrowed these books showed that students in the new Department have increased the number of science books borrowed from storage. Yale can look forward to an increased call upon "seldom-used, scholarly books" in the various branches of science as its new Department grows in strength, but it is doubtful that there will be extensive use of this class of material at the main University Library.

Use of Storage Books by Date of Publication

The analysis of the dates of publication called for from storage in two years, correlated with the distribution by predominant languages of the publications, can, we believe, be used effectively in evaluating any program for the storage of seldom-used scholarly books in a large research library. Through analysis by decade of all classes and languages of books, we discovered no trend toward increased use of books published between 1550 and 1800; no more than 25 books published in any decade during this period were called for in the two years of the study. From 1880 to 1960 the curve of use rises constantly until a peak is reached during the decade of 1951 to 1960; some 800 books published within that decade were requested from storage.

These loans, analyzed by date of publication, were studied according to use by groups of readers: faculty, graduate students, undergraduates, staff (including factories), special (visitors and paid users) and by interlibrary loans. Among these we discovered a not unexpected and fairly regular decline in the use of older books among all classes of users.

ANALYSIS OF QUESTIONNAIRES

Simultaneously with the above study an analysis was made to responses of 830 questionnaires filled out by the users. In this analysis, as in the study reported above, graduate students constituted the greatest number of users and undergraduates the second largest; these were followed by faculty, others (paid users, visitors, etc.) and library staff.

We inquired how the readers learned about the books for which they asked and found that nearly one-third of the books called for from storage were discovered by the reader himself in the public card catalogue. The proportionately small number of faculty (14.71 per cent) and of graduate students (28.16 per cent) who found books through the card catalogue seems to indicate both that they know the literature of their field and do not have to rely on the catalogue to lead them to it and also, perhaps, that they are dissatisfied with the subject headings in the Library's catalogue. This complaint, voiced on every campus, is a weakness in cataloguing that is acknowledged by the cataloguing profession. Somewhat less than half of the faculty and graduate students say that they generally find the books they want in the catalogue under the author's name, but only ten per cent of the faculty and nineteen per cent of the graduate students say that they find what they want "more often under subject entry."

On the whole, the sample demonstrated a fairly equal distribution of other sources of recommendation for particular titles among all classes of readers, with only a few variables, none of which seem significant in view of the greater importance placed on the card catalogue and bibliographies.

Selecting the Book

We asked our respondents whether they were looking for a particular book before they found that it was in the storage collection, or whether they were just looking for a book of this general nature. Fewer than twenty per cent of all readers were looking for a particular book, and only thirty-one per cent were looking for a book of the same general nature.

We went to the sources of nearly fifty replies to this query that were made by faculty and graduate students and in nearly all cases discovered that there was dislike of the book storage program based upon lack of information as to what it entailed, failure to understand anything but the most negative possibilities of such a program, and a decidedly adverse reaction to change.

Browsing

The freedom to browse in the book stacks of libraries is greatly cherished by faculty members and students in American universities, and their opposition to a storage program is largely based on the fact that it means the removal of books from open stacks to an area where they are unavailable for this purpose. They conceive of browsing in a classified arrangement of books as comparable to using a printed subject bibliography.

Browsing has been carefully and intelligently studied in the Fussler-Simon volume, *Patterns in the Use of Books in Large Research Libraries* (Chicago, 1961; pages 185-205); and we agree with the conclusions of this study, especially that "We see no completely happy reconciliation on this issue if any books are to be stored compactly. Yet we think these factors should be noted: (1) For a very long period of time, if not permanently, the majority of books in most, if not all, research libraries will stay as accessible as they are at present; only a small percentage will go to storage. (2) Those that would go to storage would be very infrequently used. (3) Furthermore, serendipitous discoveries and effective browsing can only occur if all these conditions are met: (a) if the pertinent book or information was acquired by the library in the first place; (b) the book has not been misshelved or lost, is not charged out of the library, nor in transit when wanted; (c) the reader is searching in the appropriate location within the classification scheme; and (d) the library has no books of greater pertinence located elsewhere. The complexity of the chain of events does not mean that browsing is unimportant, but it does suggest what every good scholar knows: browsing alone cannot serve as a satisfactory base for a serious literature search."

Although expert and intensive research is carried on in closed stacks libraries all over the world, both faculty and library staff at Yale feel strongly that this kind of research cannot be as effective as examination of the publications at the shelves. We in no way deny the value of browsing but should like to point out that the faculty members who assisted in weeding did find material in the stacks which they were willing to designate for storage, or even for discarding. It seems, therefore, that if faculty, students and library staff can be fully apprised of the purposes of a storage program and can understand clearly that the material removed from the stacks is of marginal value for research, there will be less opposition to such a program. Good public relations with faculty, students and staff are highly important if a library undertakes a storage program.

"I Want the Book to . . ."

A majority of readers who called for books from storage wanted to read them in their entirety, while one-quarter of the calls were to read a particular passage. Others — small percentages (under five per cent) — were for diverse reasons, such as looking at an illustration or map, checking a footnote, or providing a footnote or bibliographical reference. A few wanted to quote a passage. Nearly one-sixth of the respondents to the question offered a variety of indefinite reasons, with no discernible pattern, indicating a random approach to books which might be helpful to them.

Card Catalogue Use

Ancillary to our queries about the use of storage books, we asked readers some questions about their general use of the card catalogue for all kinds of books. A summary, based on over four hundred telephone calls or interviews in addition to answers in the questionnaires, seems to indicate that faculty know their authors, mistrust, or otherwise find inadequate, subject entries in the catalogue, recognize some titles, and to a large extent, along with graduate students and staff, find a portion of their books through direct access to the stacks. Graduate students know the authors they need to read, either by assignment or otherwise, and make greater use of the subject approach in order to help find "everything" in their fields. Graduate students, incidentally, seem to make greater use of *see* and *see also* references than do other readers, probably because of a greater desire for thoroughness. Undergraduates use the subject approach more than other classes of readers, usually in pursuit of material for assigned subject papers. Staff use of author entries is high because they often seem to have specific works in mind. Visitors and paying users were not queried by interview.

Where Will Books Be Used and For How Long?

We discovered from the questionnaires that more than half of the borrowers who called for books from storage wanted them for home use. One-sixth of the readers did not respond to this question, probably because the questionnaires were generally filled out at the time the book was requested and before the reader had a chance to see it and appraise its usefulness for his purposes. Another one-sixth of the borrowers wanted the books for only a brief period of use within the Library.

All other loans — for faculty offices, for cubicles in the stacks, etc. — equalled about ten per cent of the total. More faculty borrowed books for home use than for use in their offices, and more than one-sixth of them called for books for only a brief period of use in the Library.

VI

THE CATALOGUE DEPARTMENT
AND THE PROGRAM

INTRODUCTION

The Catalogue Department faced the advent of a greatly enlarged Selective Book Retirement Program with considerable experience in the problems involved since, as already stated, a storage program for selected new acquisitions had been in operation since 1943 and one for weeding the stacks since 1953.

In these sixteen years an arrangement of the storage collection had been designed which provided for a minimum of waste space in shelving the publications, and rules for simplified cataloguing of this material had been established. Also, a decision had been made that material in storage would be given as full subject coverage as that in the stacks except that subjects would not be assigned to an edition in the storage collection if there was an edition in the stacks or other open collection. We were well aware that the procedures for handling material selected for retirement from the stacks needed a thorough review and looked forward eagerly to having staff and time to study these and to develop more expeditious methods.

STORAGE PROGRAM PRIOR TO 1959

A brief outline of Yale's program and policies for materials in storage prior to the grant from the Council on Library Resources will make clear the base from which we started.

The Program and Its Purposes

In 1959, before the expanded program began, the Library was assigning to storage monographs, complete files of serials which had ceased publication, and long, consecutive, early runs of current serials. The purposes of the collection were outlined as:

1. To make the stacks collection more meaningful to readers by eliminating publications which are of minor value as subject matter or are out-of-date and by eliminating multiple editions.

2. To relieve crowding in the stacks.

3. To save costs of binding and rebinding and of plating, labelling and marking.

4. To eliminate the expense of classification.

Arrangement and Physical Handling of the Collection.

In the storage collection the volumes were arranged in six size groups, with those in the first four sizes shelved on their fore edges, as follows:

Shelved on fore edges:
WA up to 5 inches in width and not over 8 inches in height
WB 5-6 inches in width and not over 9 inches in height
WC 6-7 inches in width and not over 10 inches in height
WD 7-9 inches in width and not over 12 inches in height
Shelved upright:
WE 12-16 inches in height
Shelved flat:
WF 16 inches or over in height

Under each letter the titles were assigned consecutive numbers as catalogued; *e.g.,* WA   WA   WA   WB   WB   WB,   etc.
                                         1   2   3   1   2   3

The shelves were filled completely, leaving no room for insertion of additional volumes.

Each volume had its call number written on the inside of the front cover, and every tenth volume had the call number on the outside; in the first four sizes this volume was put in a box which was labelled and marked with the call number. Call numbers on the labels of volumes tranferred from the stacks were completely obliterated by use of a heavy, soft pencil, experience having shown that, if an old call number was at all readable on a storage book which is charged out, the shelvers would frequently reshelve it in the stacks rather than in storage.

There were also two separate size groups for dissertations: (1) WG up to 6½ inches in width and not over 10 inches in height, and (2) WH 7-8½ inches in width and not over 12 inches in height. Since these are largely unbound and generally rather thin, they were shelved in boxes, ten to fifteen to a box.

This arrangement had proved satisfactory and was, therefore, continued when the program was expanded.

THE PROGRAM 1959-1962

The expanded Program, as already stated, called for increasing the number of volumes weeded from the stacks each year from an average of 20,000 to approximately 60,000. The latter figure was selected because the library was adding that number of volumes per year to the collections in the main University Library and one of the objectives of the study was to learn whether the growth of a library's active collection can be stabilized by weeding as many volumes per year as are added.

The volumes selected for removal from the stacks were to be handled in five ways:

1. Transferred to the storage collection.
2. Transferred to another library within the University.
3. Transferred to a library outside the Yale system.
4. Filmed or have microfilm ordered to replace them.
5. Discarded.

In preliminary discussions between the Director of the Program and the Head of the Catalogue Department, it was agreed that faculty and staff members who did the selecting would be asked to study the books at the shelves with the shelf list in hand, marking the cards lightly in pencil as to the recommended disposal of each title in accordance with the above.

To carry out the program in the Catalogue Department, that is, the withdrawal of the volumes from the stacks after they had been selected and correcting or clearing the catalogue records, a staff of eleven was planned — three professional, two subprofessional, and six clerical assistants; two of the staff, one professional and one subprofessional, worked part time, thus making a total full-time staff of ten. At the beginning, we provided experienced personnel insofar as this was possible so that the project could get under way without loss of time for training people.

In planning routines and work flow, the Supervisor of the Program for the Catalogue Department, Frances R. Lubovitz, made every effort to concentrate in the special staff all functions connected with the withdrawal of material from the stacks in order that accurate cost statistics could be compiled. These operations had formerly been scattered according to the nature of the work. Miss Lubovitz aimed, also, to keep a steady flow of material moving from the stacks to the selected destination so that work would not backlog in one area and be slack in another.

Processing Procedures

Procedures for processing material selected for withdrawal from the stacks will vary from library to library because of the different policies and practices which are followed. It is unnecessary, therefore, to give in detail those developed at Yale. In order that cataloguers may know what such a program will mean for them, however, we give here an outline of our procedures. A manual giving the details of each routine, step by step, is available from the Yale University Library on request. The general routine is as follows:

Weeding

Weeder checks books at shelf, working with one shelf list tray at a time. (1) Marks cards lightly in pencil as follows, turning marked cards up on end:

W   (if recommended for storage collection)
D   (if recommended for discard)
T   to ＿＿＿＿＿ (if recommended for transfer to another library)
F   (if recommended for microfilming)

(2) Notes on shelf list cards volumes which need repair, rebinding or relabelling. (3) When work on a shelf list tray is completed, weeder gives it to Supervisor.

Supervisor withdraws cards and holds them until weeding of an entire subject subclass (*e.g.*, German history) has accumulated. Taking all cards in one subject subclass, she: (1) Checks them and removes any which appear to be outside the categories of material generally assigned to W. (2) Removes those for volumes needing repair, rebinding or relabelling and sends them to Head of Binding Department. (3) Refers remainder to Associate Librarian in charge of book selection, the faculty or curators for final review. When reviewing has been completed, she puts cards in tray marked "To be Photoclerked."

Photoclerking and Alphabetizing

Clerical assistant: (1) Photoclerks shelf list cards for books selected for storage to make temporary slips for filing in the catalogues in place of main entries. (2) After slips are developed, cuts them to card size and punches holes at bottom. (3) Matches slips with shelf list cards. (4) Alphabetizes cards and places them in tray marked "Books to be searched."

Searching

Cataloguing assistants search each title in the catalogue and record information on an "Added copy and/or editions" form slip, at the same time withdrawing the main entry and substituting a Photoclerked slip for it.

Distribution of Cards

Supervisor reviews searching and: (1) Divides cards into 4 groups:

    W (storage)
    D (discard)
    T (transfer to another library)
    Titles which need recataloguing

(2) Files cards for books assigned to storage in tray marked "Cards to be withdrawn." (3) Put discards, transfers and titles

to be recatalogued aside to accumulate until there are enough in each group to be processed.

Withdrawal and Arrangement of Cards

Clerical assistant: (1) Withdraws cards needed to complete the sets. (2) Arranges sets of cards in shelf list order. (3) Files cards in tray marked "Books to be collected."

> [It should be noted that up to this point no books have been collected; this is postponed until all preliminary work has been completed so that books will be available on the shelves as long as possible rather than be piled up within the work area awaiting further processing].

Collecting Books and Allocating Them to Size Groups

When about 150 sets of cards, which generally represent enough books to fill a truck, have accumulated in the tray marked "Books to be collected," clerical assistant: (1) Collects the books from the stacks on large book truck and returns with them to the work area. (2) Counts the number of volumes removed from the shelves. (3) Measures the linear footage of space cleared in the stacks in each subject subclass by measuring the books on the truck. (4) Records these figures. (5) Measures books to allocate them to size groups *(i.e.,* WA, WB, etc.); also measures newly catalogued books received from Descriptive Cataloguing Division for size. (6) Puts books on shelves allocated for these groups.

Numbering of Books

When there are enough books of one size to fill a large book truck, clerical assistant: (1) Removes books from shelves for numbering. (2) Obliterates the old call number from the book. (3) Writes new W call number in book. (4) Types new number on official catalogue main entry. (5) Inserts colored tags in volumes to be boxed, plated or labelled, indicating that this is to be done. (6) Submits truck to reviser.

Revision

During the revision, the reviser separates books from their cards.

When revision is completed, the trucks are sent to the basement to have the books boxed, labelled and marked.

Marking and Shelving

Clerical assistant boxes books, labels and marks boxes.

Circulation Department assistant shelves books and returns trucks to project area.

Counting and Distribution of Cards

Supervisor: (1) Reviews the cards and counts the number of entries and volumes processed according to whether they have been newly catalogued, recatalogued or reclassed. (2) Sends cards for newly catalogued and recatalogued books to the Card Processing Division to have sets made. (3) Puts cards requiring corrections in call numbers in tray marked *Secondary work to be done.*

Secondary Work

Clerical assistant erases stacks call number from cards and adds storage number.

Professional staff revises secondary work.

Filing

When cards are ready for filing, clerical assistant records the number of inches of cards, sorts them by first letter, and sends them to be arranged with other cards for filing in the catalogues.

Books which require recataloguing are given to the cataloguing assistants, whose work is revised by the revisers. If the entries raise problems too difficult for these subprofessional assistants, the recataloguing is done by a reviser. Books to be discarded and transferred to other libraries are processed according to the same routine as books assigned to storage, except that no temporary slips are filed in the catalogues in place of the main entries. The revision of these is done by the Supervisor.

During the entire time that the books are in process, there are no charges for them in the Circulation Department; but the Head of that Department is kept informed as to areas on which the project staff is working, and the temporary slips in the public and official catalogues have been Photoclerked with a mask which reads "W transfer" so that any queries for a particular title will be referred to the project Supervisor.

EFFECT OF THE PROGRAM ON THE
CATALOGUE DEPARTMENT

Introduction

It would seem that, with ten additional staff for this project, the Catalogue Department would be in a happy position; and in many respects this was true. But, if the cost statistics of the project were to be meaningful to other libraries, it was necessary to draw a sharp line between those parts of the work which truly dealt with the processing of the books selected for retiring from the stacks and those which resulted from our cataloguing policies or which involved procedures that went beyond the actual withdrawing of books and processing them for a recommended destination. It was inevitable that the work load of the regular cataloguing staff would be increased as a result of the movement of such a large number of books, although the segregation of all activities connected with the Program lightened it in some ways.

Withdrawal of Experienced Staff

Perhaps the greatest impact on the Catalogue Department was the withdrawal of experienced staff, especially of senior staff, who were assigned to the supervision of the project, and having to train replacements. This, coupled with additional work resulting from the project, created serious backlogs of work at times.

Increased Amount of Recataloguing and Reclassing

A second major problem was a large increase in the amount of recataloguing and reclassing. The selection of material to be retired from a collection which has existed for more than two hundred years brings forth a large number of titles for withdrawal that require recataloguing; this was inevitable at Yale, since many of the old books in the Library are still represented in the catalogues by inadequate entries on handwritten half-cards. The additional load of recataloguing, which was originally assigned to the regular staff, was far too heavy for them to handle; and very early in the project the special staff had to assume this task.

Transfers to departmental libraries within the University, for which the Catalogue Department regularly does the cataloguing, were also heavy; and, since many of these libraries do not use the main University Library classification, this frequently meant reclassing, as well as either recataloguing or adjusting the cards and making additional cards for the departmental library. At times when the transfers were extensive in number, the clearing of the records by the SBRP staff had to be correlated with the ability of the subject and descriptive cataloguers to handle the cataloguing. It should be said, however, that, because of the changing library situation at Yale, many of these books would have been transferred even if there had been no Selective Book Retirement Program; and the Department was fortunate in having extra staff to clear the records and collect the volumes.

Increased Amount of Filing

The increased amount of filing was a third major problem for the Department. With thousands of cards coming out of the catalogues each month and a large proportion of them having to be refiled after the call numbers had been changed to storage numbers, the filing load was so heavily increased that the regular filing staff could not handle it and periodically we had to assign cataloguers to filing to help catch up with the backlog. Since, however, they were already working under heavy pressure, this was not a satisfactory solution; it only helped us through emergency situations.

Most of the other problems resulted from the changing policies which have been followed in developing our catalogues through the years. Since these would vary in every library, it seems unnecessary to describe them here.

Improved Procedures

Among the beneficial results are improvements in procedures for handling withdrawals of material from the stacks, worked out by the Selective Book Retirement Program staff, which resulted in greater efficiency and increased output per man hour. An enumeration of these would mean little without an explanation of the Yale catalogues and the policies governing them that make certain procedures necessary. An explanation of a few of the changes will, however, indicate the direction they took.

Probably the greatest improvement came from centralizing all processes in one staff group and making a sharp division between the professional and clerical aspects of the work. This saved considerable time for the professional staff and made it possible to keep the cost of processing the material withdrawn from the stacks at a low level. The concentration of the work in one group also made it unnecessary to make charges in the Circulation Department for the books in process, as explained earlier.

The routines for the various procedures, as described in the manual which Miss Lubovitz prepared, reflect more specific changes, some of which relate only to the handling of books being retired from the stacks and others of which are applicable to the regular work of the Department. In the former group are a faster method of measuring books for size and allocating shelves for the various size groups so that the books can be sorted when brought from the stacks and will not have to be handled a second time for this purpose. In the second group are a faster method of withdrawing cards from the catalogues, which increased the average number of sets withdrawn per hour from 10.7 to 13.5; a speeding up of secondary work by assigning two clerical assistants to work together as a team, which increased the average output from 10.5 sets per hour to 15.6; development of form slips for making requests for standard information.

Many of the changes seem minor; but, when applied to thousands of books, they add up to a major saving of time. It should be stressed, therefore, that if a library undertakes a program of this kind, every step of every procedure should be studied carefully to ferret out each part of the operation that is inefficient.

PROBLEMS TO BE CONSIDERED

The program pointed up two problems of procedure for the Catalogue Department which should be considered in planning the future development of the Selective Book Retirement Program at Yale.

Transfers to Storage from School Libraries

The first is the handling of transfers to storage from the major school libraries, which do their own cataloguing. Yale's present procedures call for withdrawal of the publications from the school library and the absorption of the material in the main University Library's storage collection. This process is both expensive and not very satisfactory for the school libraries. This is due to two factors: first, since the school libraries (Divinity, Law, Medical and Music) use special subject heading lists, all transfers have to go through the hands of the subject cataloguers in the main University Library for assignment of subject headings, and they also have to be handled by descriptive cataloguers to prepare a card for use in the central library; second, the school library maintains no record of these transfers, thus losing an approach through their catalogues to this material.

The Head of the Catalogue Department believes, therefore, that, if the Selective Book Retirement Program is continued at Yale, a change should be made in the procedures for handling material weeded from these libraries. She recommends that consideration be given to providing a storage area which is large enough so that each of the four major school libraries can have its own storage section and can transfer volumes from its collections as it is able to weed them. These publications would probably not be shelved in compact storage but would retain their present call numbers with "Storage" stamped above the call numbers on catalogue cards. This would mean not only that each library would process its own volumes, but that it would retain a record in its catalogue, both under author and subject, of the material. It would also obviate the necessity for the recataloguing and reassignment of subjects by the Catalogue Department in the main University Library. Some of the saving in expense of processing would be transferred to increased storage costs, but the departmental library would be more satisfied since it would retain bibliographical control of the material.

Microfilming

The second procedural problem relates to microfilming. Although it was expected that the project would result in extensive microfilming of bulky publications and of materials in poor condition, this result was not achieved. This was due in part to the fact that the Library had been involved in the substitution of microtexts for bound volumes for six years, and many of the most obvious candidates for such a program had already been handled, namely, long files of newspapers and folio-sized periodicals on poor paper.

A second reason was, however, the difficulty in developing a coordinated policy for making decisions on the kinds of publications that should be microfilmed and those for which the Library should not spend money. Filming is not the solution for replacing books in poor condition if they are in heavy use, and it is inadequate for publications with any illustrations, especially double page and colored ones. Monographs approved for filming accumulated so slowly that the project staff did not attempt to process them until the Program was about ended, since a decision had been made not to send monographs for filming until enough pages had accumulated to fill, or nearly fill, one reel.

Serials presented different problems. Faculty members were prone to recommend incomplete files of periodicals for filming; these the librarians could not approve for they realized that incomplete files are frustrating to users and that the high cost of microfilming an incomplete file cannot be amortized by selling copies of the film to other libraries. If the serial was important, investigation was made to find out if a film were already available; but, as explained earlier, more often than not the serial had never been filmed and the cost of having one copy made was prohibitively expensive.

The lack of success in this area has pointed up the need for a well coordinated program for microfilming of materials in the Yale Library.

SUMMARY

The expanded Selective Book Retirement Program brought problems to the Catalogue Department, as can be seen in the preceding report; but, in viewing it as a whole, the Department administrators cannot but realize that the Library's collections, its catalogues, and the Catalogue Department have gained immeasurably from it. Many publications that were an impediment to efficient use of the stacks collection have been removed, and those areas which have been weeded are in much better condition than those still to be done. The catalogues of the Library have been cleared of hundreds of handwritten and poorly catalogued entries, and the cards withdrawn for discards and transfers to other libraries have helped to stem the growth of the catalogues. The opportunity to think through and experiment with methods of handling publications to be withdrawn from the stacks has resulted in improved procedures that will assist the Department for years to come, and the codification of many nebulous policies for weeding, applicable to new acquisitions as well as to the stacks collection, will be a great boon to the Department work.

VII

CATALOGUE DEPARTMENT STATISTICS

During the almost three years of the Selective Book Retirement Program the Catalogue Department kept detailed statistics of every phase of the operations: the number of volumes handled and the disposition of the volumes, the number of volumes and titles catalogued, recatalogued and reclassed, the amount of space cleared in the stacks, the number of boxes used. It also kept statistics of the time spent in each operation and from these computed the cost of each phase of the work and the average cost of handling a volume in this Program.

Detailed statistics are on file at the Yale University Library. The following tables summarize the essential ones.

VOLUMES WITHDRAWN FROM STACKS AND DISPOSAL OF THEM

	Monographs	Serials	Pamphlets	Total
Transferred to storage	41,933	14,238	16,234	72,405
Transferred to other libraries	7,109	8,184	1,966	17,259[1]
Discarded	6,695	11,087	10,661	28,443
Total withdrawn	55,737	33,509	28,861	118,107

Total space cleared: 8,984 feet, 6½ inches

[1] Of these 2,572 volumes were sent to libraries outside the University.

CATALOGUING STATISTICS
(VOLUMES ADDED TO STORAGE COLLECTION)

	Monographs	Serials	Total
New cataloguing[1]	13,157	1,031	14,188
Recataloguing	6,079	1,076	7,155[2]
Reclassing	53,027	14,466	67,493[2]
Total	72,263	16,573	88,836

Linear footage of books added to storage: 6,021 feet, 7½ inches

[1] The cataloguing of new acquisitions for the storage collection is done by the regular staff of the Catalogue Department. During the last year of the Program, however, the special staff catalogued many new theses which the regular staff could not handle.

[2] The figures of volumes recatalogued and reclassed do not quite match those for volumes withdrawn from the stacks. The explanation is that the volumes withdrawn from the stacks are counted at the time they are removed from the shelves; the recataloguing and reclassing are counted at the time the volumes are numbered for storage. There is always a time lag between these two.

STATISTICS OF CLERICAL WORK

	Number of sets of cards	Number of exposures
Withdrawing	83,809	
Secondary work	53,937	
Photoclerking		95,777

TIME SPENT AND COSTS

	Hours: Minutes	Cost
Professional Staff	12,450:10	$33,080.60
Subprofessional staff	8,367:30	12,098.40
Clerical staff	28,344:15	36,757.60
Total	49,161:55	$81,936.60

In addition to the above time spent on processing material selected for removal from the stacks, staff members spent varying amounts of time on tasks which were not part of the processing procedures. This resulted from several situations: (1) the regular staff of the Department was too busy to handle the work promptly (*e.g.*, cataloguing of newly received theses); (2) a lull in the weeding made the work slack in the project, thus freeing the staff for other tasks; (3) staff emergencies in other parts of the Library led to the assignment of a staff member to cover the situation temporarily (usually at times of severe storms). The professional staff also spent considerable time in assisting with the weeding during the last two years of the project; although this was project work, it cannot be included in the processing costs.

The following table indicates the time spent on work other than processing of material selected for weeding from the stacks:

	Hours: Minutes	Cost
Professional staff	575:10	$1,497.87
Subprofessional staff	189:15	278.35
Clerical staff	296:15	388.64
Total	1,060:40	$2,164.86

All but 202:30 hours ($531.61) was for work directly connected with the project, but not processing.

Processing Cost per Volume

In computing cost per volume of processing the weeded material, we have used the following figures:

	Volumes
Catalogued, recatalogued and reclassed for storage	88,836
Transferred to other libraries	17,259
Discarded	28,443
Total	134,538

The number of volumes catalogued, recatalogued and reclassed for the storage collection was used in preference to the number removed from the shelves, because this is the actual number of volumes that were added to the storage collection during the period of the project and includes the newly catalogued volumes as well as those transferred from the stacks.

The total cost of the processing part of the program, $81,936.60, divided by the number of volumes handled, 134,538, gives a total processing cost per volume of $.609, or, in round figures, $.61 per volume.

VIII

YALE COMPACT STORAGE

Four and one-half times as many books can be shelved by the Yale Compact Storage Plan as in conventional stack arrangement. The Yale Plan utilizes standard double-faced bookstack sections 7'6" in height with 22" aisles. The books are shelved by size and on the fore edge (for sizing see page 36). By conventional stack arrangement or shelving is meant the use of standard double-faced bookstack sections with 36" aisles and classified book order with capacity figured at 250 volumes per double-faced section.

The per volume cost for books shelved according to the Yale Plan is 42 cents. The per volume cost for conventional shelving is $1.68. These figures were arrived at by comparing building costs of a structure yielding an area of 8,300 square feet on one floor level and include the cost of steel bookstacks at currently prevailing prices. The volume count per square foot is: Yale Plan 64, conventional 14.

Other stack types and plans were also compared with the basic conventional stack arrangement. These are (1) standard double-faced bookstack sections with aisle spacings of 22" and 28"; (2) mobile stacks; (3) the compact-case storage system; and (4) the drawer-type bookstacks. In order, the per volume costs range from $1.31 to $2.09 and the volume count varies from 14 to 30 per square foot. If the Yale sizing scheme is introduced in these plans, the order remains the same, although an increased capacity factor should be added to the volume figures.

Experience at Yale has demonstrated that any of these aisle widths is practical; the narrow aisles are being used daily by faculty, students and Library staff alike.

MOBILE STACKS

A special study was made of the feasibility and utility of mobile stacks. Since no installation in libraries is known, except for office-library situations, two types of mobile stacks were installed and studied. The first consisted of a pre-fabricated nylon castered base movable in metal tracks imbedded in a plywood floor. Standard double-faced bookstack sections were fastened into these movable bases. The second type, by a different manufacturer, consisted of standard double-faced bookstack sections with nylon casters or wheels affixed to the base of the bookstack section itself, but again operated on metal tracks imbedded in a plywood floor. The first type costs twice as much as the second type, which costs $130 per double-faced section.

The per volume cost for mobile stacks is $1.45 (figured at the lower installation cost) with twenty-one books shelved per square foot of space as compared with $1.69 per volume for stationary conventional stacks and 14 volumes per square foot. Utilizing Yale's sized arrangement, the comparison remains in the same order.

Mobile stacks are easy to use providing the double-faced bookstack sections are perfectly balanced and the floor is level. The stacks can be put into motion with one hand and without the exercise of undue strength. Yale employs girls as pages in the bookstacks. These young ladies were able to move the mobile units without strain, experiencing greater difficulty only in overcoming the initial inertia of the fully loaded double-faced sections. In both installations stops and bumpers were employed to prevent damage to the books from collisions or the overturning of a mobile double-faced bookstack section.

Our studies and experience indicate, however, that in spite of the ease of use and increased capacity of books per square foot of floor space, mobile stacks are not practical for library installations. It would seem they are more practical and economical for office-type libraries where floor space costs are high, thus justifying the increased cost of the casters, track, and plywood flooring.

The summary chart and the seven stack plans which follow are an attempt to present visually the results of book storage studies at Yale. The figures used have been computed by dividing the gross book capacity, area and cost figures as shown on the plans. All figures are rounded to the closest whole number for the sake of quick reference and, therefore, are not exactly divisible as if they were carried out to four decimal points. In using the figures it must be remembered that there will be variations due to local building codes, supply and demand, and competitive bidding. The constants used in the calculations are also important since any variations in these will directly affect the cost figures. However, the relative order of capacities and costs will remain the same.

From the Yale studies it can be concluded that the more useful comparative figure of those presented in planning book storage is the per volume cost figure as related to the different types of book stacks and the different aisle spacings.

SELECTIVE BOOK RETIREMENT PROGRAM
Constants Used In Calculations

Building		Stacks
Construction	Brick and Concrete	Free Standing Bracket Type
Size	8300 Sq. Ft.	7'6" high
Module	24'5" x 28'4"	36" plate shelves
Estimated cost	$20.00 per Sq. Ft.	10" closed bases
No air conditioning		8" adjustable shelves
Aisle lighting included		No end panels

REFERENCE		CONVENTIONAL		YALE SIZED COMPACT	
		Per Vol.	Per Sq. Ft.	Per Vol.	Per Sq. Ft.
Plans 1 and 4	Cost	$1.31	$24.56	$ .42	$26.11
22" aisles	Capacity		19 v.		64 v.
Plan 2	Cost	$1.47	$23.97	$ .47	$25.40
28" aisles	Capacity		16 v.		53 v.
Plan 3	Cost	$1.69	$23.39	$ .52	$24.70
36" aisles	Capacity		14 v.		41 v.
Plan 5	Cost	$2.09	$60.48	NOT APPLICABLE	
Drawer Type	Capacity		30 v.		
36" aisles					
Plan 6	Cost	$1.69	$46.73	$ .78*	$68.04*
Com-Pac-Case	Capacity		28 v.		88 v.
36" aisles					
Plan 7	Cost	$1.45	$31.27	$ .45*	$33.05*
Mobile Stacks	Capacity		21 v.		72 v.
36" aisles					

Note — By reversing layout and increasing length of ranges capacity could be increased approximately 2% in Plans 1, 2, 3, and 4.

*No field experience.

PLAN 1-22' AISLES

USING

3'-6" STACK RANGE SPACING
7'-6" STACK HEIGHT
10" BASE SHELVES
6-8" SHELVES ABOVE BASE

STORAGE AND COST DATA

SIZE OF BUILDING- - - - -97'-8" × 85'-0"
SIZE OF MODULE- - - - -24'-5" × 28'-4'
AREA - - - - - - - - - -8301 SQ. FT.
BOOK CAPACITY- - -155,250 VOL.
WORKING CAPACITY PER DOUBLE
FACED SECTION- - - -250 VOL.
621 DOUBLE FACED SECTIONS
NUMBER OF BOOKS PER SQ. FT.- - - -19
ESTIMATED DELIVERED COST PER
DOUBLE FACED SECTION- - - -$61.00
ESTIMATED BUILDING COST PER
SQ. FT.- - - - - - - - - - -$20.00

BUILDING COST- - - - - - -$166,020.00
STACK COST- - - - - - - -$37,891.00
TOTAL COST- - - -$203,911.00

COST PER VOLUME- - - - - -$1.31
COST PER SQ. FT.- - - - - -$24.56

NOTE—NO SPACE ALLOWED FOR WORK
ROOM, STAIRS OR TOILETS. ADD
APPROXIMATELY 20% TO AREA FOR
THESE FACILITIES, ASSUMING BUILDING
WILL NOT BE OVER 4 FLOORS IN HEIGHT.

85'-0"

97'-8"

24'-5"

28'-4"

3'-6"

3'-0"

1'-10"

21'-0"

3'-5"

18'-0"

3'-10"

PHOTOGRAPHIC REDUCTION: 64.6%

SCALE - 1/8" = 1'

56

PLAN 2 - 28" AISLES

USING-

4'-0" STACK RANGE SPACING
7'-6" STACK HEIGHT
10" BASE SHELVES
6-8" SHELVES ABOVE BASE

STORAGE & COST DATA

SIZE OF BUILDING - - - - 97'-8" × 85'-0"
SIZE OF MODULE- - - - - 24'-5" x 28'-4"
AREA- - - - - - - - - - 8301 SQ.FT.
BOOK CAPACITY   135,000 VOL.

WORKING CAPACITY PER
DOUBLE FACED SECTION-- 250 VOL.

540 DOUBLE FACED SECTIONS
NUMBER OF BOOKS PER SQ.FT.- - -16
ESTIMATED BUILDING COST
PER SQ. FT.- - - - - - - - - - $20.00
ESTIMATED DELIVERED COST
PER DOUBLE FACED SECTION- -$61.14

BUILDING COST- - - - - - - -$166,020.00
STACK COST - - - - - - - - -$33,018.00
          TOTAL COST- - - - $199,038.00

COST PER VOLUME- - - - - - - - $1.47
COST PER SQ. FT.- - - - - - - - $23.97

NOTE-NO SPACE ALLOWED FOR WORK
ROOM, STAIRS OR TOILETS. ADD
APPROXIMATELY 20% TO AREA FOR
THESE FACILITIES, ASSUMING BUILDING
WILL NOT BE OVER 4 FLOORS IN HEIGHT.

97'-8"

85'-0"

24'-5"

24'-5"

24'-5"

24'-5"

28'-4"

28'-4"

28'-4"

2'-7"

21'-0"

21'-0"

21'-0"

16'-0"

2'-4"

4'-0"

3'-5"

3'-5"

3'-5"

3'-0"

3'-10"

PHOTOGRAPHIC REDUCTION: 64.6%

SCALE 1/8=1'

57

PLAN 3 -36" AISLES

USING

4'-8" STACK RANGE SPACING
7'-6" STACK HEIGHT
10" BASE SHELVES
6-8" SHELVES ABOVE BASE

STORAGE AND COST DATA

SIZE OF BUILDING- - - - -97'-8" × 85'-0"
SIZE OF MODULE- - - - -24'-5" × 28'-4"
AREA- - - - - - - -8301 SQ. FT.
BOOK CAPACITY- - -115,000 VOL.
WORKING CAPACITY PER DOUBLE
FACED SECTION- - - -250 VOL.
459 DOUBLE FACED SECTIONS
NUMBER OF BOOKS PER SQ. FT.- - -14
ESTIMATED BUILDING COST
PER SQ. FT.- - - - - - -$20.00
ESTIMATED DELIVERED COST PER
DOUBLE FACED SECTION- - -$61.32
BUILDING COST- - - - - - -$166,020.00
STACK COST- - - - - - $28,145.00
    TOTAL COST- - - -$194,165.00
COST PER VOLUME- - - - - - -$1.69
COST PER SQ. FT.- - - -$23.39

NOTE-NO SPACE ALLOWED FOR WORK
ROOM, STAIRS OR TOILETS. ADD
APPROXIMATELY 20% TO AREA FOR
THESE FACILITIES, ASSUMING BUILDING
WILL NOT BE OVER 4 FLOORS IN HEIGHT.

85'-0"

97'-8"

24'-5"

28'-4"

9'-0"

3'-0"

3'-5"

21'-0"

18'-0"

12"

3'-10"

PHOTOGRAPHIC REDUCTION: 64.6%

SCALE-1/8"=1'

PLAN 4-22" AISLES

USING

3-6" STACK RANGE SPACING
7-6" STACK HEIGHT
10 BASE SHELVES
8' - SHELVES ABOVE BASE

YALE COMPACT STORAGE
ALL BOOKS SIZED FOR STORAGE
STORAGE AND COST DATA

SIZE OF BUILDING – – – – –97'-8" x 85'-0"
SIZE OF MODULE – – – – – 24'-5" x 28'-4"
AREA – – – – – – – – – 8301 SQ. FT.
BOOK CAPACITY – – –522,000 VOL.
621 DOUBLE FACED SECTIONS
NUMBER OF BOOKS PER SQ. FT. – – 64
CAPACITY BASED ON FOLLOWING
SHELF SPACING:
25% 14 SHELVES HIGH PER SECTION
50% 12 SHELVES HIGH PER SECTION
20% 10 SHELVES HIGH PER SECTION
2% 8 SHELVES HIGH PER SECTION
3% 5 SHELVES HIGH PER SECTION
ESTIMATED BUILDING COST
PER SQ. FT. – – – – – – –$20.00
AVERAGE COST PER DOUBLE FACED
SECTION – – – – – – – –$81.73
BUILDING COST – – – – – –$166,020.00
STACK COST – – – – – –$50,752.00
            TOTAL COST – –$216,772.00
COST PER VOLUME – – – – – –$.42
COST PER SQ. FT. – – – – – –$26.11
NOTE: NO SPACE ALLOWED FOR WORK
ROOM, STAIRS OR TOILETS. ADD
APPROXIMATELY 20% TO AREA FOR THESE
FACILITIES. ASSUMING BLDG. WILL NOT BE
OVER 4 FLOORS IN HEIGHT.

97'-8"

85'-0"

SCALE – 1/8"=1'

PHOTOGRAPHIC REDUCTION: 68.6%

59

PLAN 5-36" AISLES
STOR-MOR BOOK DRAWERS

USING

7'-6" STACK HEIGHT
14 DRAWER UNIT = 2 DOUBLE FACED
SECTIONS OF STACK, 8" DEPTH STORAGE
THROUGHOUT.

STORAGE AND COST DATA

SIZE OF BUILDING — — — — — — 97'-8" × 85'-0"
SIZE OF MODULE — — — — — — — 24'-5" × 28'-4"
AREA — — — — — — — — — — — —8301 SQ.FT.
WORKING CAPACITY PER 7 DRAWER
UNIT—DOUBLE COMPARTMENT—250 VOL.
NUMBER OF BOOKS PER SQ. FT. — — —30
ESTIMATED BUILDING COST PER SQUARE
FOOT — — — — — — — — — — — $20.00
960 - 7 DRAWER UNITS—DOUBLE
COMPARTMENT, ESTIMATED DELIVERED
COST PER UNIT — — — — — — — —$350.00
BUILDING COST — — — — — — —$166,020.00
STACK COST — — — — — — — —$336,000.00
              TOTAL COST— — — — — $502,020.00

COST PER VOLUME — — — — — — —$2.09
COST PER SQ. FT. — — — — — — —$60.48

NOTE: NO SPACE ALLOWED FOR WORK
ROOM STAIRS OR TOILETS. ADD
APPROXIMATELY 20% TO AREA FOR
THESE FACILITES ASSUMING BUILDING
WILL NOT BE OVER 4 FLOORS IN
HEIGHT.

PHOTOGRAPHIC REDUCTION: 64.6%

SCALE 1/8" = 1'

85'-0"

97'-8"

PLAN 6-36" AISLES
COM-PAC-CASE STORAGE SYSTEM
USING
7'-6" STACK HEIGHT
8" BASE SHELVES
6-8" SHELVES ABOVE BASE
STORAGE AND COST DATA

SIZE OF BUILDING – – – – – – – 97'-8"×85'-0"
SIZE OF MODULE – – – – – – –24-5" × 28'-4'
AREA – – – – – – – – – – – –8301 SQ. FT.
BOOK CAPACITY – – – – – –230,000 VOL.
NUMBER OF BOOKS PER SQ. FT. – – –28
ESTIMATED BUILDING COST
PER SQ. FT.– – – – – – – – – $20.00
297–3'-0' DOUBLE FACED SECTIONS
      STATIONARY AT $66.00 EACH
54 – 3'-0' WALL SECTIONS
      STATIONARY AT $49.50 EACH
648–3'-0 DOUBLE FACED SWING
      SECTIONS AT $308.00 EACH
BUILDING COST– – – – – $166,020.00
STACK COST – – – – – – $221,859.00
      TOTAL COST $387,879.00
COST PER VOLUME– – – – – – $1.69
COST PER SQ. FT. – – – – – – $46.73
NOTE: NO SPACE ALLOWED FOR WORK
ROOM, STAIRS OR TOILETS. ADD
APPROXIMATELY 20% TO AREA FOR
THESE FACILITIES. ASSUMING
BUILDING WILL NOT BE OVER 4
FLOORS IN HEIGHT.

97'– 8"

85'-0"

24'-5"

21'-0"

3'-5"

4'-0"

7'-0"

3'-0"

28'-4"

24'-5"

18'-0"

3'-10"

DIVISIONS FOR ALL RANGE UNITS SAME AS SHOWN ABOVE

PHOTOGRAPHIC REDUCTION: 64.6%

SCALE 1/8"=1'

61

PLAN 7 - 36" AISLES
MOBILE STACKS
USING

BANKS OF (2) 3'-0" STACK SECTIONS
7'-6" HIGH STACK ON BALL BEARING
ROLLERS.

10' BASE SHELVES
6-8" SHELVES ABOVE BASE

STORAGE AND COST DATA

SIZE OF BUILDING--------97'-8" 85'-0"
SIZE OF MODULE-------- 24'-5" 28'-4"
AREA --------------- 8301 SQ.FT.
BOOK CAPACITY------------180,000 VOL.
WORKING CAPACITY PER DOUBLE
FACED SECTION-----------250 VOL.
717 DOUBLE FACED SECTIONS
NUMBER OF BOOKS PER SQ.FT.---21
ESTIMATED BUILDING COST PER
SQ.FT.-------------------$20.00
ESTIMATED DELIVERED COST PER DOUBLE
FACED MOBILE SECTION-----$130.46
BUILDING COST----------$166,020.00
STACK COST-------------$93,540.00
         TOTAL COST---$259,560.00

COST PER VOLUME-------- $1.45
COST PER SQ.FT.-------- $31.27
NOTE: NO SPACE ALLOWED FOR
WORK ROOM, STAIRS OR TOILETS.
ADD APPROXIMATELY 20% TO AREA FOR
THESE FACILITIES, ASSUMING
BUILDING WILL NOT BE OVER 4 FLOORS
IN HEIGHT.

PHOTOGRAPHIC REDUCTION: 64.6%

SCALE 1/8"=1'

85'-0"

97'-8"

IX

CONCLUDING STATEMENT*

by

RAYMOND P. MORRIS, *Librarian*
YALE DIVINITY SCHOOL

In terms of long range perspective, responsible judgment suggests that there is no feasible choice before libraries other than a wide and continuous program of selective book retirement. This is imposed upon us because shelf space is limited and ultimately our space in libraries will be filled. We should not, of course, rule out the possibility of further adaptation of other campus space, but moves in this direction should never be made until their cost has been carefully examined and all other possibilities considered and fully exploited.

If the judgment is sound that selective retirement of books is a necessity imposed by the growing size of libraries, we shall be wise to meet this problem when it can be done apart from a sense of crisis and pressure resulting from book shelves already filled to the full and overflowing. We shall learn better from planned experience which reflects actual situations and includes theoretical projections rather than from "crash programs".

The ultimate objective of the selective retirement of books should be to cope with the problem of shelf space with as little detriment to library resources and program as possible. It is of utmost importance that we assess, as clearly as we can, the effects of what we are attempting to do. No one will like selective retirement in all of its features, and it is possible, through an unwise application of it, to render grave damage to book collections. The

*Edited by Lee Ash from a letter of May 28, 1962

action taken must reflect sound judgment. It "goes against the grain" of many people whose judgment we respect, to contemplate discarding materials of historical evidence which, in fact, is quite a different matter from what we mean by selective book retirement. We are proposing to transfer materials of secondary importance to the fundamental purpose of our work to other collections in the University, or to compact storage. It is important that all concerned understand what we are doing, that we do not underestimate the value of historical record, that we minimize irreparable damage to our collections. This is our responsibility as custodians, as librarians, as a University in our society. It is important that we understand the undesirable results, or even the sheer impossibility, of our libraries continuing indefinitely to follow an acquisition program along the principle of exhaustive historical documentation (keeping everything) comprehensively applied to all or even to a wide range of subject areas. Such acquisition programs are necessary or may be required in certain areas; they cannot and they should not be applied to all areas. It is important to note that no American university library system has been able to gather the resources to support a broadly defined, unrestricted acquisition program which does not employ or envisage, ultimately, a selective book retirement feature.

Acquisition policy and selective book retirement are two aspects of one problem, and it is folly to consider one apart from the other. American university libraries have been able to bail themselves out of this dilemma through lavish expenditure of money. We have not given the attention to this matter of acquisition which it requires. We can, in turn, simply use selective book retirement as the most feasible way to undo the damage done through unwise acquisition programs. The ultimate problem is both selective acquisition and selective book retirement.

Our experience suggests that a program of selective retirement of books can be effected, probably in any of our university library collections, in a manner that will not result in undue damage to our book collections. It would be unwise, and perhaps dishonest, to claim that we can pursue a plan of selective retirement with no damage to our collections. In many important aspects, however, selective book retirement stands to improve and strengthen the usability of a book collection by enabling us to continue, unimpaired, other important library services and functions. An unrestricted acquisition program with no selective book retirement feature can smother the efforts of the library so that other important educational efforts and services are seriously neglected.

It should be made unmistakably clear, then, that selective book retirement does not mean recklessly discarding or destroying material and data which we have no competence to evaluate, or which cannot be assessed fully in our generation. Selective book retirement is segregating material which we intend to keep in a manner that will be less expensive for the University. The service based upon a selective book retirement program will be as generous as the library can afford, and as good or better than that which our European and some other friends have, or ever have, enjoyed. Therefore, we believe, that at Yale a selective book retirement program is not only an inescapable conclusion to any long-range consideration of the problems of books and space, but, if we can be carefully discriminating, it bids well to offer improved library services. Indeed, its consideration can lead to a strengthening of our acquisition policy in terms of quality. The program is, frankly, still experimental and our judgment must be tentative.

It is of the utmost importance that we continue to explain to the faculty and to the university community what we are doing, that our academic community be accurately informed, that we secure participation (insofar as this is possible) in our efforts, that we solicit and benefit from their criticisms. We need constant and constructive criticism from interested university personnel. Faculty judgment is a necessary check to be used in the execution of the program, though this judgment must, in turn, be confirmed and held in check by librarians who, by training and experience, are more familiar with the library's total acquisition plan. Generally, our experience suggests that the opinions of individual faculty members, in selecting books for retirement, are too restricted in interest, too specialized in knowledge, and lacking in their grasp of the whole situation. Although faculty judgment is indispensable in the execution of such a project, it should not be definitive.

A selective book retirement program can be effected in a number of ways. It can be determined in a large university system that an entire class or body of literature is so infrequently used or marginal to the foreseeable purposes of the university, that, as a compromise, it be transferred to retirement in a storage area. This, in principle, simply means that we choose to use our most desirable equipment for the most important purposes. It has the distinct advantage of simplicity and, therefore, can be more easily effected; furthermore, it maintains bibliographical control at all necessary points.

In the actual process of selection for a book retirement program, we have found very little that can be reduced to a formula or routine. A library may be able to follow a formula, in part, by carefully delineating the areas which are to be permanently included in the collection. This is more easily done for a school or departmental collection, but there is no reason why it could not be done for an entire university library. Material in areas where we do not intend to collect in depth, or to keep for permanent record, can be retired as it becomes obsolete in terms of the needs of school or department. Related to this is a constant updating of those sections of materials required in instruction. This feature, however, represents but a small fragment of the total acquisition program of the library and does not, therefore, really get at the matter.

Beyond this, the execution of selective book retirement becomes increasingly a matter of knowledge, judgment and wisdom. It may be too simple to say that we shall retire the less important edition or the stereotype edition when we have an earlier or critical edition, or one that is somewhat better. This again reflects only a minor fragment of the task to be done. Ultimately, for the purposes of genuine selective book retirement, the matter resolves itself into a continuous assessment of the probable value of material to a subject discipline, both for now and for the future. This cannot be determined solely on the basis of its use. We know of no simple rule or canon which can be applied in arriving at this judgment. For example, there is no way for selective book retirement to be effected in the Divinity Library without permanent damage to the collection if selection is done apart from a deep and wide knowledge of Theology in its various aspects and the material which will be required to support its understanding. The implications are clear in terms of the qualities of judgment and the type of personnel which will be required to do this work.

It follows that a program of choosing for the selective retirement of books will be expensive to implement. Our experience demonstrated that it is the most difficult aspect of our work to execute. It requires the most competent of our personnel in terms of knowledge and experience. If one does not know what he is doing the whole matter seems easy. But, when done in a truly responsible way, such as we envisage, it is time-consuming, requiring the best judgment that we can muster, which means that it is an expensive program. It could very well turn out that it will prove so expensive in execution that (as with microreproduction) there will be a point beyond which it will not be feasible in terms of economy. Any library can evaluate this problem, we believe, but only through experience and not through theorizing.

It is also clear that to be successful selective book retirement must be a program executed over an extended period of time. It must become as routine as acquisition and other recognized library procedures. It cannot be executed successfully as a "crash program". One implication would be that we should expect to increase our permanent staff, which would mean larger administrative budgets.

We do not believe that selective book retirement will be fully successful, or that it will be accepted by our academic community, until we have developed it as an integral part of adequate bibliographical control. We must assume that material placed in compact storage loses much of its reference value to a library. Bibliographical controls, including adequate cataloguing, must be effected to minimize this loss. Further, unless such control is maintained, one cannot develop a collection of strength and depth. Not enough attention has been given to this aspect of this project.

Selective book retirement, like many other things, is not a panacea nor a completely satisfactory solution. We should not expect it to resolve our library space problems. We believe that it can be a useful device to delay and to retard the development of a major library problem, and in such a manner that a university library can accommodate itself to the terrific problem of the preservation, care and maintenance of material reflecting this top-heavy civilization of which we are a part. We should like to take the next ten years learning, in part, how this might be done.

APPENDICES

Selective Book Retirement Program: Purposes and Policies

Catalogue Department Routine: Extracts from the *Manual of Procedures*

DEFINITIONS

SELECTIVE BOOK RETIREMENT PROGRAM

The Selective Book Retirement program is a program of systematic weeding the stacks, class by class, and of the school and departmental libraries to select volumes to be retired from the libraries' open collections. The volumes may be:

1. Assigned to the storage collection (W).

2. Transferred to another library at Yale which has the major responsibility for the subject field.

3. Transferred to a library outside of the Yale system.

4. Filmed or have microfilm ordered to replace them.

5. Discarded.

STORAGE COLLECTION

The storage collection is a closed stack collection arranged by size and within each size numerically as catalogued. It is shelved in compact storage, with no space left for adding volumes.

The storage collection includes publications selected from new acquisitions as well as from the stacks, and the selection policies given below apply to new acquisitions as well as to material weeded from the stacks.

PURPOSES

SELECTIVE BOOK RETIREMENT PROGRAM

1. To make the stacks collection more meaningful to readers by eliminating publications which are out-of-date or of minor value as subject matter and by eliminating multiple editions.

2. To relieve crowding in the stacks.

3. To transfer to school and departmental libraries material which, according to present acquisitions policies, belongs in those libraries.

STORAGE COLLECTION: ADDITIONAL PURPOSES

1. To eliminate the expense of classification [for new acquisitions].

2. To save costs of binding or rebinding and of plating, labelling, and marking.

SELECTION POLICIES

GENERAL

The policies given below are not hard and fast but are to be considered as guides to selection of material for withdrawal from the stacks. In all cases judgment must be used.

Weeders must be continually cognizant of important titles and editions in the fields under consideration and of the editions that should be retained in the stacks.

Weeders must be aware that material is important, not just to its primary subject field, but also to related fields, and must consider the cross-subject interests of the faculty.

Titles in subject areas which are of particular interest to the Yale Library or in which the Library has a special collection are not discarded but may be assigned to W if of minor importance to the Yale collection.

Titles dealing with subjects on which there is very little material available are preferably retained in the stacks.

Weeders should remember that the storage collection is not a "wastebasket" for material in too poor condition to circulate, since books in W are available for circulation. Such material should be recommended for replacement or filming if needed in the Library.

If it can not be replaced and the original needs to be preserved, it may be transferred to W.

All material that is being withdrawn from the collections in the main University Library (i.e., for discarding or transferring to another library) must be referred to the Associate Librarian in charge of book selection for final decision in order to have a more consistent approach to a policy.

STORAGE COLLECTION

Types of Material Which Are Generally Assigned to W

1. Out-of-date scientific and technological material.

2. Out-of-date travel guides unless there is no other edition at Yale.

3. Transfers from L & B [undergraduate browsing collection] which have not circulated in three years.

4. Books on highly specialized topics which are covered or duplicated in more extensive studies.

5. Books in uncommon languages (Finnish, Hungarian, Polish, etc.) on very specific topics and on general topics which are not of special interest to Yale (e.g., Agriculture, Domestic Science).

6. Farmington acquisitions in German and Swiss dialects.

7. Farmington acquisitions of a technical nature (how-to-do-it books).

8. Inspirational literature.

9. Juveniles [not all juveniles are kept; see Acquisitions policy for juveniles].

10. Non-contemporary minor authors.

11. Elementary and secondary school textbooks. Only a representative collection is kept, however; others are discarded.

12. Crank literature.

13. Biographies of obscure persons.

Types of Material Which Should Be Considered for W

1. Personal narratives of war experiences.

2. Transfers from departmental libraries.
N.B. When the departmental library is a working collection and the main University Library has the research collection (*e.g.*, Chemistry, Engineering), books should be considered for W or stacks on the same basis as our regular collections.

3. Early imprints which are not wanted in special collections.

4. Out-of-date books in any field.

Material Which Should Not be Classed in W

1. British Tracts, *i.e.*, pamphlets printed in Great Britain between 1641 and 1800 inclusive and phamphlets published elsewhere which relate to Great Britain or her colonies in general. [These class in British Tract files].

2. Theological writers before 1800. [These class in Mhc].

3. British and American individual sermons of any period. [These class in sermon files or in British Tracts].

4. Quaker tracts. [These class in Quaker tract files in M].

5. Pamphlets which require binding or boxing to shelve in W.

6. Monograph continuations which are still being published.

TRANSFERS TO DEPARTMENTAL LIBRARIES

General

Departmental libraries at Yale fall into two categories:
Category 1. The major school libraries which have the responsibility for the research collection in their subject field.

These are:
- a. Divinity Library.
- b. Forestry Library.
- c. Law Library.
- d. Medical Library.
- e. Music Library.

Category 2. The libraries of departments of the University (e.g., Chemistry, Physics), which are working collections only. In these subject areas the main University Library has the responsibility for the research collection in the field.

Policies for Transferring Material to:

Category 1: Major school libraries

The responsibility for the subject fields of the libraries in this category is assigned as follows:

Divinity Library: Responsibility divided; see Acquisitions policy memorandum no. 3.

Forestry Library: Primary responsibility to Forestry Library. Theses on forestry in storage collections in main University Library.

Law Library: Primary responsibility to Law Library. Main University Library acquires collections of law needed for reference (e.g., U. S. Statutes at large) and laws pertaining to special fields as needed.

Medical Library: See Acquisitions policy memorandum no. 2.

Music Library: Music Library orders books for both libraries and decides on location.

Publications which are within the areas of responsibility assigned to these libraries are sent to those libraries for decision as to location.

Exceptions:

1. Standard works in a field; *e.g.,* biographical directories,

bibliographies, encyclopedias, histories; these may be classed in the stacks or reference collections in Sterling.

2. Publications which are needed for class use or reserve shelves; these may be classed in the stacks or the Reserve Book Room.

3. Important works by members of the Yale faculty. *N. B.* Publications not wanted for the stacks or other open collections are sent to the school library; they are not assigned to W.

Duplicates of editions in these libraries are discarded unless:

a. There is a clear need for a title in the main University Library.

b. The departmental library has requested that all duplicates be sent to it.

N. B. A duplicate of a book in one of these libraries is not assigned to W; if needed, it is classed in the stacks or other open collection.

Exception: Travel books in Divinity Library (Day Missions Collection).

Variant editions of titles in these libraries are sent to the Library holding the title.

Exception: Travel books in Divinity Library (Day Missions Collection).

Category 2: Smaller Libraries

Transfers are made to the libraries in this category only with the approval of the librarian of the departmental library. This is necessary because these libraries have very limited space.

Transfers Requested by a Departmental Library

Requests from a departmental librarian for the transfer of specific titles are referred to the Assistant Librarian in charge of departmental libraries for decision.

DISCARDS

Material Which is Generally Discarded

1. Student course outlines, except Yale.

2. Correspondence school material.

3. Accessions lists of general libraries. [If from special library and of subject value, they are kept.]

4. Press releases.
   > Exceptions: Yale releases (files in Yale Memorabilia Room).
   > U.S. Government releases (current issues are kept in Reading Room for a limited time).

5. Publications of colleges or universities (*except* Yale, Harvard, and Oxford) in the following categories:
   a. Newspapers.
   b. News bulletins.
   c. Newsletters.
   d. Press releases.
   e. Humor magazines.
   f. Literary magazines edited by students.
   g. Scattered files of programs.
   h. Non-current books of views.
   i. Alumni publications that are news bulletins only.

6. Programs of meetings.

7. Speeches of officers of corporations published for purposes of advertising.

8. Speeches of government officials.

9. Publications dealing with dentistry.

10. Publications dealing with veterinary medicine.

Material That Should Be Considered for Discarding

1. Publications on subjects in which Yale has little or no interest; these are retained only if considered important to a

research collection, are of interest to other fields, or are needed for general use. Included are:

   a. Agriculture.
     Historical, economic and social material is retained.
   b. Domestic science.
     Material that reflects the customs of a country is retained.
   c. Education.
     Historical material, material on higher education, and most publications relating to Connecticut are retained.

2. Reprints (*see* below under *Pamphlets* and *Dissertations*).

3. Mystery and detective fiction; only a representative collection of the best writers is retained.

See also below under Copies, Editions, Practical duplicates.

Pamphlets

Pamphlets are generally not assigned to W since: (1) The Library has subject pamphlet boxes in the stacks, and the processing of a pamphlet is less expensive if it is added to one of these than if handled as a monograph in W. (2) Pamphlets are unbound and often thin and flimsy. They, therefore, require boxing or binding to be shelved on their fore edges in compact storage; otherwise they are likely to be damaged.

Any pamphlet which is assigned to W must be one which is essential for the Library's permanent collection, since W is not weeded as pamphlet boxes in the stacks are.

Pamphlets which are covered by more permanent published material (books, periodical articles, etc.) are discarded.

Pamphlets which are ephemeral or out-of-date are discarded, but weeders must watch for those which are bibliographically important (*e.g.,* Confederate imprints), are important as a subject contribution, are early publications or printings of an important author, or are the chief material available on a topic.

Dissertations

Dissertations are assigned to W with the following exceptions:
(1) A dissertation in a subject pamphlet box which has a date due slip showing that the volume is frequently used is retained in the stacks. (2) A dissertation which seems to be a major contribution to a subject field is catalogued and classified as a monograph in the stacks. (3) A dissertation on an individual literary author is generally classified with the author, particularly if it is an author which Yale collects. Exceptions may be made for minor authors. (4) An abstract of a dissertation which is a reprint from a periodical which Yale has or an abstract which consists of only a title page and brief summary is discarded.

Copies

General rule. In general, 2d copies which are no longer needed are not assigned to W but discarded. Occasionally 2d sets of heavily used periodicals or, more rarely, of copies of monographs may be assigned to W for preservation because we know that we shall have to replace them.

Two copies classed in different locations. If searching shows that a title being considered for W has a 2d copy in a classed-together series, the classed individually copy is discarded rather than assigned to W.

> *Reason:* If it is so little used that it is not needed with other materials on the same subject, there is no justification for putting it in an unclassified arrangement in storage since the catalogue will direct readers to the copy classed with the series.

Added copies in Reserve Book Room. If searching shows that there is another copy of an edition being considered for W in the Reserve Book Room, the book should be retained in the stacks rather than be assigned to W.

> *Reason:* Yale's policy is to have a circulating copy in the stacks of material in the Reserve Book Room.

Thesis vs. trade editions. If searching shows that Yale has both the thesis and trade editions of a title and the contents are *exactly* duplicated, the copies are compared and, conditions being equal, the thesis edition is discarded.

Practical Duplicates

Practical duplicates are copies of a title which are exact reprints except for:

1. The date of publication *or*

2. The place of publication (usually published in different countries, as New York and London editions).

> *Please note:* Collation must always be identical. An illustrated edition is not a duplicate of one which is not illustrated, nor is one with black and white plates the same as one with plates in color.

Until about ten years ago practical duplicates were catalogued on separate cards. Yale now catalogues them as added copies, and they should be so considered.

Copies are compared and the one in poorer condition discarded rather than assigned to W. In general, English editions of English authors are kept, American editions of American authors, etc.

Editions

If there are two or more editions of a work and the later editions are revised and expanded, the latest edition is kept in the stacks and earlier editions are considered for W or discarding.

Editions in more than one language. (1) Original language edition and English translation, if there is one, are assigned to the stacks. Translations into other languages are assigned to W. (2) If the original edition is in a difficult language and there is no edition in English, the original and the most easily read translation (French, German, Spanish, Italian) are assigned to the stacks. (3) Translations of works originally published in English are assigned to W if Yale has the English original.

Prolific Authors

Inexpensive reprint editions (A. L. Burt, Grosset & Dunlap, etc.) are discarded rather than assigned to W.

If author is one which Yale collects, editions are sent to Associate Librarian in charge of book selection for decision.

Duplicates in Special Collections

If searching indicates that there is an exact duplicate in a special collection, the copy is sent to Associate Librarian in charge of book selection for decision. If the decision is that a second copy is needed, it is kept in the stacks.

Books That Have Been Charged to Reserve Book Room Recently

If there is any indication on date due slip that book has been on reserve within the last five years, book is retained in stacks rather than transferred to W. Book may be needed again for Reserve Book Room.

Heavily Used Material

If a book has been charged out on an average of once a year or more for the past five years, it should be considered "heavily used" material and should not be transferred to W.

Serials

Rules given above that are applicable to serials may be followed. The rules given here are additional rules that apply to serials only.

Serials that should be considered for W.
1. Complete files of titles which have ceased publication.
    a. If set has a cumulative index, the index is retained in the stacks.
2. Early volumes of long current serial sets.
    a. Although no hard and fast rule can be made as to

the length of an early file to be transferred, in general not less than 50-60 volumes should be transferred. The reasons are: (1) The transfer must save sufficient space in the stacks to justify the work of changing the records, and (2) A serial main entry card has room for no more than three call numbers, and only two are preferable. Therefore, if a set is to be split, enough of it should be transferred at one time so that it will not be necessary to continue adding call numbers to the cards, as would be required if the volumes were moved in small segments.

3. Incomplete serial sets or incomplete early files of current sets may be transferred if ten per cent or less of the title is wanting.

a. Boxes are inserted in place of missing volumes so that there will be room to shelve the volumes if they are acquired later.

Serials that should be considered for discarding. (An attempt should be made to offer these to libraries lacking our volumes).

1. Titles of which Yale has only one or two volumes unless checking shows that this is all or nearly all that has been published.

2. Very incomplete or scattered files, particularly if there are very few or no complete volumes (*i.e.,* Yale has only a few issues of several volumes).

3. Juvenile periodicals.

Analyzed monograph series which are classed together. Classed together analyzed monograph series are generally not transferred to W because of the work required to change the call numbers on the analytic cards. They may be transferred if: (1) Analytics are unnecessary according to present practice and can be cancelled (these are chiefly page analytics). (2) Space saved in stacks is so extensive that it justifies the work of changing the analytic cards. (3) Call number has to be changed, anyway; for example, sets which are classified in old classifications that the Library is clearing out. (4) Yale has only a few volumes of the series, in which case the series entry is changed to "classed individually" and the volumes are handled as monographs.

SUBJECT POLICIES FOR W PUBLICATIONS

Publications in W are given as full subject coverage as those in the stacks. Subjects are important since the books cannot be located through classification. The following rules apply:

1. Avoid general subjects if more specific ones can be assigned.

2. Eliminate subject if the publication is one which would ordinarily be approached by author; *e.g.,* publications which are of interest chiefly because of the organization which issues them.

3. Assign no subjects if there is an edition in the stacks.

CATALOGUE DEPARTMENT ROUTINES

Extracts from the *Manual of Procedures*

The following extracts from the Manual of Procedures, prepared by Frances R. Lubovitz, are included to show some of the improved methods developed that would be applicable in other libraries.

CARD WITHDRAWAL

The withdrawal of one complete set of cards at a time by a clerical assistant results in his having to retrace his steps around the catalogue repeatedly. A plan for systematic withdrawal of cards alphabetically was devised to eliminate this inefficiency, as follows:

Clerical assistant:

1. For monographs: Withdraws official catalogue main entry. (Public catalogue main entry was withdrawn by searcher during searching process).

    (a) If it has no tracings so that there are no secondary entries to be withdrawn, he files set behind the metal follower in his filer's box. If the official catalogue main entry is a black photocopy, tracings will be found on public catalogue main entry.

2. For serials: Withdraws public catalogue main entry and holdings card. (Serial catalogue main entry and holdings cards for incomplete serials were withdrawn by serial reviser during searching process).

3. Files sets with tracings behind alphabetical guide cards, filing each set under the tracing which is first in the alphabet.

4. Withdraws cards indicated in tracings from public catalogue, each time refiling set under the tracing next in alphabetical order until sets are complete.
   (a) Those sets with added entries which have to be withdrawn from the official or serial catalogue, are left standing on end.
5. Returns to official or serial catalogue and completes withdrawal of sets.

MEASURING AND SIZING OF VOLUMES

Prior to the expansion of the Selective Book Retirement Program under the Council on Library Resources Grant, volumes designated for storage were accumulated indiscriminately on a large table and sized individually with a ruler when it appeared that a sufficient number of volumes of one size was available to fill a book truck. This was a slow and cumbersome procedure and made it difficult to locate a particular volume, should the need arise. The following plan was devised to facilitate the handling, sizing and sorting as a combined operation.

1. In measuring volumes to be shelved in W (storage), the terms used are height and width.

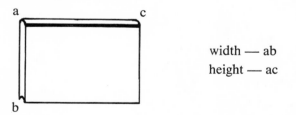

width — ab
height — ac

2. Volumes are measured according to the dimensions listed below:

Shelved on Their Fore Edges:
   WA — up to 5 inches in width and not over 8 inches in height

WB — 5-6 inches in width and not over 9 inches in height

WC — 6-7 inches in width and not over 10 inches in height

WD — 7-9 inches in width and not over 12 inches in height

Shelved Upright:

WE — 12-16 inches in height

Shelved Flat:

WF — 16 inches or over in height

[Shortly after the project began, the use of WF was discontinued in general, since Circulation Department reported that folio size volumes are difficult to handle in the narrow aisles in the storage area.]

3. Clerical assistant measures volumes for W (storage) at table equipped with measuring device on which are designated size limitations for WA-WD. He slides each book separately against device which is made with two ¾-inch-boards fastened at right angles to each other (see illustration below). The spine of the book is fitted against side A and the top of the book against side B.

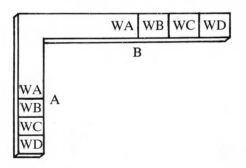

4. He piles books on table which is marked off with sections for each size.

5. When table is filled, he puts books on shelves designated for each size. These shelves are located along the wall in the work area.

BOXING, LABELLING, MARKING

1. Boxes are available in four sizes and in four colors; all boxes of one size are the same color so that sizes can be recognized easily. Each size is available in fifteen widths from ¼″ to 4″.

WA — 5″ high — 8″ long — green
WB — 6″ high — 9″ long — red
WC — 7″ high — 10″ long — tan
WD — 9″ high — 12″ long — black

2. Volumes to be boxed are indicated in two ways: *i.e.,* by a brightly colored tag saying *Box Label Mark* [used to indicate tenth numbered volume or each first volume of a title in multiple series] or a tag saying *Box* [used for volumes in poor condition].

3. Clerical assistant. (a) Writes call number on gummed labels for volumes tagged *Box Label Mark* (WA-WD) or *Label Mark* (WE-WF). The labels come in sheets. Lettering is done with India ink and a pen with a B6 penpoint. (b) Selects proper size box and inserts volume in box. (c) Removes gummed labels from sheets and attaches them to closed end of box.

Top

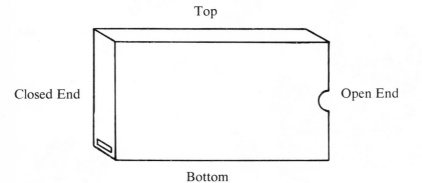

Closed End   Open End

Bottom

(d) Returns volumes to correct location on truck.

4. Volumes in sizes WE and WF having the tenth numbers are labelled and marked on the lower part of the spine of the book, but not boxed.

FORM SLIPS AND SHEETS

Various form slips and sheets were developed (1) to simplify work directions, (2) to maintain a statistical record of time spent on each phase of the operation, and (3) to record the number of volumes actually processed in a given time.

Form slips. In the first category are the *Direction Slip for Secondary Work* and the *Direction Slip for Serial Secondary Work*. *N.B.* The direction *Withdraw* is used when a set of cards which has been withdrawn is found to be incomplete. Card withdrawal is not revised until the revision of the numbering process. This eliminates handling the cards twice and any missing cards can be searched by the clerical assistant when he does the secondary work on a set of cards.

DIRECTION SLIP FOR SECONDARY WORK

Type .... card

Remove stamp:

Stamp over call number:

Type call no. in top call no. position:

Remove call number(s):

                                     — — Dash entry

Withdraw: Initials:

DIRECTION SLIP
FOR SERIAL SECONDARY WORK

Type .... card

Remove stamp:

Stamp over call number:

                     date

On serial history card add vol no. to top call number:

Type W call no. in lower call no. position:

Remove call number(s):

                           — — Dash entry

Withdraw: Initials:

The *Added Copies and/or Editions Slip* is used during the searching process. At this time the searcher indicates the Library's pertinent holdings of a title and gives directions for the transfer of tracings.

ADDED COPIES AND/OR EDITIONS

cat   Location

cat   Location

Cancel tracing for W copy

Make tracings for:

Please be careful to note copies classed in different locations, copies in Reserve Book Room, thesis or trade editions, virtual duplicates.

Time sheets. In the second category are time sheets for each grade of personnel with the exception of the Supervisor. They give a clear picture of the diversification of the responsibilities within each grade, the division of professional and clerical work, and the over-all scope of work entailed in such a program. *N.B.* Some assignments are repeated at the professional and clerical levels in order to accommodate (1) the advanced clerical assistant who is capable of doing some of the semi-professional work, and (2) the time when all grades of personnel are required to work at any phase of the operation in order to complete a particular assignment within a specified time. Time spent doing work in various departments of the Library and on weeding is recorded separately in order to deduct the labor cost from the program budget.

SBRP report of: Reviser's time sheet
Period:

Date	A	B	C	D	E	F	G	H	I	J	K	L	M	N	O	Total

A — Snags   I — Recataloguing
B — Revision of recataloguing   J — Miscellaneous
C — Revision of numbering   K — Sick leave and vacation
D — Revision of secondary work   L — Work in Serial Department
E — Revision of marking   M — Work in Rare Book Room
F — Proofreading   N — Catalogue Department filing
G — Searching   O — Weeding
H — Non-productive work

SBRP report of: Cataloguing assistant time sheet
Period:

Date	A	B	C	D	E	F	G	H	I	J	K	L	M	N	O	P	Total

A — Recataloguing
B — Searching
C — Non-productive time
　　　(relief, meetings, etc.)
D — Proofreading
E — Snags
F — Revision of serial clerical work
G — Discarding serials
H — Reviewing sets of serials

I — Miscellaneous
J — Sick leave and vacation
K — Revision of numbering (theses)
L — Withdrawing
M — Filing
N — Catalogue Department filing
O — Transfer of serials
P — Revision of secondary work

SBRP report of: Clerical assistant time sheet
Period:

Date	A	B	C	D	E	F	G	H	I	J	K	L	M	N	O	P	Q	R	Total

A — Withdrawing
B — Secondary work
C — Collecting books
D — Sizing
E — Searching missing vols.
F — Numbering books
G — Photoclerking
H — Boxing, labelling, marking
I — Filing
J — Measuring vols. in stacks

K — Non-productive time
　　　(relief, meetings, etc.)
L — Searching
M — Typing temporary slips
N — Miscellaneous
O — Sick leave and vacation
P — Erasing call nos. from books
Q — Catalogue Department filing
R — Alphabetizing photoclerk sets

Statistics of work. In the third category are sheets for recording work completed. Two sets of figures were kept to record volumes and entries processed. *Volumes Withdrawn from Stacks and Space Cleared* were recorded by subclass each time volumes were removed from the stacks for transfer to storage or another library or were removed for discarding. *Volume and Entry Statistics* refer to the actual number of volumes and entries processed for storage. They include new cataloguing [done by the Descriptive Cataloguing Division] and divide the transfers from the stacks into those which were recatalogued and those which were only reclassed. All volume and space cleared figures were compiled for a quarterly report. Volume and time statistics were then used to compute the labor cost of each phase of the operation and the cost of processing a single volume.

SBRP report of: Volumes withdrawn from
Period: stacks and space cleared
Subclass:

Volumes to W		Space cleared				Volumes discarded		Space cleared			
Monograph	Serial	Monograph	Serial			Monograph	Serial	Monograph	Serial		
Vols.	Vols.	Ft.	In.	Ft.	In.	Vols.	Vols.	Ft.	In.	Ft.	In.

SBRP report of: Volume and entry statistics
Period:

W cataloguing		W recataloguing		W reclassing	
Vols.	Entries	Vols.	Entries	Vols.	Entries

Volumes withdrawn from stacks and space cleared

					Space Cleared			
	Monographs	Serials	Pamphlets	Total	Monographs	Serials	Pamphlets	Total
Transferred to W								
Transferred to other libraries								
Discarded								
Total								
Transferred to W								
Transferred to other libraries								
Discarded								
Total								
Transferred to W								
Transferred to other libraries								
Discarded								
Total								
Grand Total								
Transferred to W								
Transferred to other libraries								
Discarded